75757

W9-BWI-852

World Chronology Series

GERMANY

A CHRONOLOGY AND FACT BOOK

1415-1972

Compiled and Edited by
ROBERT VEXLER

1973
OCEANA PUBLICATIONS, INC.
Dobbs Ferry, New York

Library of Congress Cataloging in Publication Data

Vexler, Robert I
  Germany: 1415-1972

  (World chronology series)
  "Documents": p.
  Bibliography: p.
  1. Germany--History--Chronology. 2 Germany--
History--Sources. 3. German--History--Bibliography.
I. Title.
DD175.V49   943   73-7792
ISBN 0-379-16305-5

Manufactured in the United States of America

To my wife Francine

without whose help
and inspiration this
book could not have
been written

TABLE OF CONTENTS

EDITOR'S FOREWORD

The World Chronology Series is intended both as an informative series for the public and a research tool for the student, consisting of basic data, pertinent documents and a critical biography. The volumes in this series should serve well as complements to the ethnic series covering emigrants from the various countries of the world.

The material presented in this volume on Germany is intended to present the basic facts necessary to an understanding of the development of the German nation. The data has been selected to illustrate the continuous growth of the concepts which contributed to the development of the state which has been so much involved in the international problems which have plagued the world during the past half-century.

The documents have been selected and condensed to indicate the basic issues and developments of German history. The works listed in the sources section of the Bibliography will provide additional original and public material. The other works selected in the Bibliography are those which will provide students with a basis for initiating detailed studies of periods in German history since the seventeenth century.

Robert I. Vexler
Briarcliff College

CHRONOLOGY

PRUSSIA, AUSTRIA AND THE GERMANIC EMPIRE

1415	Hohenzollern Dynasty transplanted from South into Mark Brandenburg, establishing itself successfully in 15th century against strong internal opposition, but played no important part in affairs of Empire.
1618	Electoral Brandenburg accepted Duchy of Prussia from Poland. May 18. "Defenestration of Prague" in which Royal Governors were hurled out of window by Protestant leaders, not seriously hurt. Initial step which led to outbreak of Thirty Years' War.
1619	Elector of Palatinate, Frederick, elected King of Bohemia. February 16. Frederick William born in Berlin.
1620	Duke Maximilian and his General, Count of Tilly, defeated Bohemians at Battle of White Mountain.
1622	Catholic League army completed conquest of Palatinate.
1629	Emperor Ferdinand II (1619-37) proclaimed Edict of Restitution providing that all church lands and dioceses which had become Protestant since Peace of Augsburg, 1555, were restored to Catholic Church.
1630	June. Beginning of third or Swedish period of 30 Years' War opened when King Gustavus Adolphus of Sweden landed in Germany.
1631	September 17. Battle of Breitenfield, near Leipzig, fought between Count Tilly and Gustavus in which Swedes annihilated Tilly's army.
1632	November 16. Battle of Lutzen in which Swedes were victorious but Gustavus Adolphus was killed on the field.

1635   May. Brandenburg joined Emperor, Elector of Saxony,
                and others in concluding Peace of Prague modifying Edict
                of Restitution, setting 1627 as date of possession of
                church holdings.

1640   December 1. Elector George William died, succeeded
                by Frederick William the "great".

1644   New army formed in which men swore oath exclusively
                to Elector of Brandenburg.

1648   October 24. Peace of Westphalia signed consecrating
                essential independence of German states. France and
                Sweden received imperial territories and became mem-
                bers of Diet.

1650   June 26. Second Congress of military men at Nuremberg
                indicating stages by which Swedes to receive their indem-
                nity.

1653   August 5. Brandenburg Diet granted Frederick William
                530,000 thaler over six-year period for upkeep of army.
                Elector promised to consult with the Estates on serious
                political issues. Frederick William bound self not to
                change method of taxation and recognize rights of nobility.

1655-   During War against Sweden, army greatly expanded and
1660   placed under single command of Field Marshal von Span.

1656   January. Treaty of Konigsberg signed. Frederick
                William forced to take Prussia as fief from Sweden.

                June. Treaty of Marienburg signed. Frederick William
                was promised slices of Poland in return for his partici-
                pation in war against Poland.

                July 28-30. Battle of Warsaw in which Frederick William
                and Charles X conquered city.

                November. Treaty of Laibau completed. Frederick
                William recognized as sovereign ruler of Prussia by
                Charles X Augustus of Sweden in return for former's
                support of Sweden when Emperor Ferdinand III inter-
                vened on side of Poland.

1657   April 2. Death of Emperor Ferdinand III led to inter-
                regnum because son succeeded him in death. Second son
                was eventually elected Emperor.

                September 19. Treaty of Wehlau. Poland recognized
                Elector's sovereignty in Prussia. In return, Frederick
                William agreed to military cooperation with Poland and
                then German Emperor against Sweden.

1658   August. Rheinbund formed by Archbishops of Mainz,
                Cologne, and Trier to promote their interests as against
                those of Emperor - - was tool of France.

1660   May 3. Peace Treaty of Oliva ended war against Sweden
                under pressure of Cardinal Mazarin of France. Freder-
                ick William denied acquisition of West Pomerania but
                his sovereignty in Russia was confirmed.

1662   Frederick William called conference of representatives
                of Calvinists and Lutherans at Berlin to end pulpit war-
                fare and possibly doctrinal disagreement.

1663   Frederick William issued edict that knights had to re-
                deem military service they owed.

1664   Frederick William issued edict forbidding all name-call-
                ing from Brandenburg pulpits, requiring all pastors of
                both confessions to prove submission in writing or for-
                feit appointment.

1666   November. Sweden required to acknowledge status of
                Bremen as free, self-governing city.

1667   Prussian towns allowed to collect their tax quota through
                an excise system, primarily tax on consumption, as well
                as on land and trade.

1672   May. France, Cologne and Munster declared war on
                Netherlands to whom Frederick William was allied.

                June. Alliance arranged between Frederick William and
                the Emperor. 16,000 imperial troops and 12,000 men of
                Brandenburg defend Imperial frontiers. Campaign was
                announced against Cologne, not against French.

1673   June 6. Peace of Vossem signed in Louis XIV's head-
                quarters near Louvain. Frederick William promised to
                end support of the Netherlands but reserved his rights
                and duties as prince of Empire.

1674   July. Frederick William admitted to anti-French alliance.

1675   January. Swedes invaded Brandenburg. Frederick
                William negotiated with Emperor and rulers of the Neth-
                erlands and Denmark for assistance.

                July 28. At Battle of Fehrbellin, Frederick William
                attacked Swedes, inflicting many casualties on them,
                although they managed to retreat to Pomerania.

1678   August. Peace of Nijmwegen concluded. Louis XIV
                offered to evacuate the Netherlands and favorable trade
                treaty.

                November. Frederick William became ruler of all of
                Pomerania.

1679   February. German Emperor concluded peace with
                France and Sweden, leaving Frederick William alone in
                war against the two states.

                June 29. Frederick William signed Peace of Saint-Ger-
                main-en-Laye, restoring West Pomerania to Sweden in
                return for minor Swedish concessions.

                October 25. "Close Alliance" (Engere Alliance) signed
                between Frederick William and Louis XIV. In return for
                ten-year guarantee of all Elector's territories, Frederick
                William granted French troops free passage through his
                lands and in his fortresses. Elector also promised to
                oppose election of member of House of Austria as Roman
                King or Emperor. Louis XIV offered 10 year annuity of
                100,000 livres enabling Frederick William to maintain
                his armaments at high level.

1683   July. Turks laid seige to Vienna, capital of German
                Emperor.

                September 12. 65,000-man army under supreme com-
                mand of John Sobieski went to Vienna and defeated Turks.

1684   August 12. 20-year armistice concluded at Regensburg
                between France and Empire leaving Louis XIV all his
                "reunited" territories and Strasbourg.

1685   November 8. Frederick William issued Edict of Potsdam
                in response to French revocation of Edict of Nantes in
                October 1685, offered Frenchmen of Reformed-evangeli-
                cal faith retreat in Prussia.

1686   March. Secret defensive alliance between Emperor and
                the Great Elector providing for mutual military coopera-
                tion and resistance to violations of rights of the Empire.
                Elector to support imperial claims to Spanish inheritance,
                aid in defense of Spanish Netherlands, and vote for Em-
                peror's son as his successor. In this 20-year alliance
                Emperor agreed to subsidize Brandenburg army.

                April. Strong Brandenburg contingent went to Hungary
                where it participated with great credit in siege and con-
                quest of Budapest.

1687   December 9. Coronation of Joseph, son of Emperor
                Leopold, as King of Hungary, indicating creation of new
                Austrian Empire. Magyar estates renounced right of
                election as long as there was male heir in Habsburg
                family.

1688   May 9. Elector Frederick William died, succeeded by
                Frederick III.

                September 24. Louis XIV issued declaration against
                Empire demanding destruction of fortifications of
                Phillipsburg, financial settlent of claims of Duke of
                Orleans against the Palatinate, and confirmation of
                William Egon von Furstenberg as Archbishop of Cologne.

                October 18. Emperor Leopold I issued war manifesto
                against Louis XIV.

1689   May. "Great Alliance" formed between Austria, the
                Netherlands and England. Austria recognized William III
                (of Orange) as King of England in return for promise of
                maritime powers to support Austrian claims to Spanish
                throne on death of Charles II as well as agreement to
                succession of Archduke Joseph to German throne.

1691	Transylvania absorbed into Habsburg Empire.

1692   Creation of new Electorate for House of Guelf obtained by Ernest Augustus of Hanover for himself and his heirs in order to redress balance in which Catholics had majority among electors.

1697   May. Opening of Peace Conference of Ryswick. Louis XIV granted favorable trade agreement to Netherlands and withdrawal of French support from James II and the Jacobites.

September 20. England, the Netherlands, and Spain signed Peace of Ryswick. Empire agreed on October 30.

1698   England, the Netherlands and France concluded first Treaty of Partition of Spanish Habsburg lands. Joseph Ferdinand to receive Spain, the Spanish Netherlands and colonies; France to gain Naples and Sicily; Milan to go to Empire.

1699   Joseph Ferdinand died.

Treaty of Karlowitz signed. Turks gave up all of Hungary and Transylvania except Banat of Temesvar.

Actual foundation of Danubian Empire of the Habsburgs created.

1700   Gottfried Wilhelm Leibnitz (1646-1716) persuaded Elector Frederick III to establish Berlin Academy of which he became President.

Spring. Second Treaty of partition of Spanish dominions: Spain, the Netherlands and the colonies to Archduke Charles, second son of Emperor Leopold; Naples, Sicily, Sardinia and Milan to France. Treaty rejected by Vienna.

October 29. Renewal of alliance of 1686 between Prussia and the Empire which also sealed Emperor's approval of Frederick's title of King.

November 1. Charles II of Spain died. Louis XIV had Philip proclaimed King. The latter arrived in January 1701 and was acclaimed by most Spaniards.

1701   January 18. Frederick III placed a new crown on his
head and that of his wife, Sophie Charlotte.

September. "Grand Alliance" of the Emperor, England
and the Netherlands signed at The Hague granting the
Emperor's just claim to the Spanish Netherlands, Milan,
Sicily and other Spanish Islands in the Mediterranean.
The Maritime powers demanded the guarantees of freedom
of trade and other colonial advantages.

1704   August 13. Battle of Blenheim, called Second Battle of
Hochstadt in Germany. Duke of Marlborough's victory
liberated all of Germany forcing French to retire behind
the Rhine.

1705   May 5. Emperor Leopold I died, succeeded by Joseph I
(1705-1711). Joseph had high conception of the imperial
dignity.

1709   September 11. Battle of Malplaquet in which 100,000
allies fought 90,000 Frenchmen forcing them to retreat.
Was only a Pyrrhic victory.

1711   April. Sudden death of Emperor Joseph I who had two
daughters – heir was brother Charles III of Spain, leading to reappraisal of political scene.

August. Force of Russians, Poles and Saxons crossed
Prussian territory on way to besiege Strasland and Wismar in spite of Prussian protests.

October. Agreement on preliminary terms in regard to
division of Spanish inheritance: Philip V (Bourbon) to
retain Spain and her colonies while renouncing for self
and heirs all claims to French throne. French Bourbons
to give up their interests in Spanish throne.

1712   January. Opening of Peace of Utrecht: Emperor Charles
VI isolated by Britain and France because he opposed
settlement by partition of Spanish inheritance. United
Provinces given to the Spanish Netherlands to be passed
on to Emperor after he agreed to limitations on his sovereignty including closing of Scheldt River to commerce.

1713   February 25. Frederick I died, succeeded by Frederick William I.

April 11. Peace of Utrecht signed by England, France, the Netherlands, Savoy and Prussia. War continued between the Empire and France until March 6, 1714, when Charles VI and Louis XIV signed Peace of Ratstatt.

April 19. Pragmatic Sanction agreed upon. Publicly announced 1718. Emperor Charles VI free to change succession in favor of his male and female offspring, removing two daughters of Joseph. All Estates consented to Pragmatic Sanction by 1732.

June. Regent of Sweden, Christian Augustus of Holstein-Gotterp concluded treaty with Frederick William. Prussian and Holstein troops to occupy Stettin, Wismar and other Swedish possessions to secure their neutrality until peace concluded.

August. Frederick William issued edict regulating affairs of royal domains only letting them out on short terms.

October 6. Frederick William concluded Convention of Schwedt with Russian General Mentschikov arranging for occupation of Pomerania by Prussians to keep neutral and prevent Swedes from using it as base to attack allies.

1714   Summer. Frederick William I concluded secret treaty with Peter the Great of Russia.

September. Peace of Baden ended War of the Spanish Succession.

1723   Johann Sebastian Bach (1685-1750) settled in Leipzig.

1726   October. Austro-Prussian Treaty signed. Developed into full alliance with Treaty of Berlin, December 23, 1728. Both governments pledged mutual support on European affairs. Frederick William I recognized Pragmatic Sanction.

1730   August 11. Prince Frederick arrested by his father, Frederick William, because of former's attempted flight. The King feared for his own life and forced Frederick to witness execution of his friend, Lieutenant Hans Hermann von Katte.

| 1733 | Stanislaus Leszczynski, father-in-law of Louis XV, elected King of Poland, defeating Frederick August III, candidate of Russia and Austria. Troops of latter nations marched on Poland prompting France, Spain and Sardinia to declare war on Austria. |

September. Frederick William divided Prussia into cantons to which regiments were assigned for recruiting purposes.

| 1739 | September 18. Peace of Belgrade signed ending Austria's war with Turkey. Western Wallachia, Servia and Belgrade passed under Turkish rule. War costly and failure for Austria. |

April 5. Cardinal Fleury concluded secret treaty with Prussia guaranteeing Prussia part of Julich-Berg inheritance.

| 1740 | May 31. Frederick William I died, succeeded by Frederick II. |

September 12. Frederick met Voltaire.

October 26. Charles VI, last male Habsburg Emperor, died.

December 16. First Prussian troops marched into Silesia, part of beginning of War of the Austrian Succession.

| 1741 | April 10. Battle of Mollwitz, first fought between Austria and Prussia. Prussian victory won by Field Marshal Schwerin. |

May 18. Treaty of Nymphenburg signed. France pledged to support Bavarian claimant to Imperial Throne.

May 28. Marshal Belleisle of France negotiated treaty by which Spain and Bavaria, principal claimants to Habsburg heritage, settled on respective shares.

June 5. Franco-Prussian Treaty concluded in Breslau. Frederick was promised Lower Silesia, and was to vote for Elector Charles Albert of Bavaria as Emperor.

June 19. Maria Theresa left for Pressburg to be crowned with Crown of St. Stephen. Promised Hungarian estates autonomy, laying groundwork for future Austro-Hungarian Dual Monarchy.

July 31. Bavaria seized Passau.

September 11. Franco-Bavarian army occupied upper Austria.

October 9. 'Convention of Klein between Frederick II and Austrian Commander, Count Neipperg. Lower Silesia to go to Prussia. Neipperg permitted to lead army un-molested into Bohemia. Convention was breach of alli-ance with France. Frederick later repudiated treaty when allies made rapid progress in Bohemia.

November. Bavarians, French and Saxons conquered Prague. Charles Albert declared self King of Bohemia.

1742   January 24. Charles Albert unanimously elected Emper-or. Same day Austrian troops entered Munich and soon occupied all of Bavaria.

May 10. 300,000 Austrians at Saar moved on Prague to cut in between Frederick and French forces under de Broglie and to attack former before reinforcements arrived.

May 17. Frederick won victory at Chotusitz showing his ability as army commander. Led to arrangements for peace.

June 11. Preliminary Peace of Breslau signed.

July 28. Peace of Berlin concluded. Frederick II granted all of Silesia, except Jugerndorf and Troppau. Deserted his allies when saw could get what wanted from Maria Theresa. Great Britain acceded to peace on Sep-tember 7.

October 7. Bavarians reoccupied Munich.

November 28. Treaty of Mutual Guarantee between England and Prussia signed at Westminster.

1743   August 24. Pragmatic Army crossed Rhine and moved to
                Worms by August 29.

                September 13. Treaty of Worms signed binding Charles
                Emmanuel of Sardinia to Britain and Austria. Maria
                Theresa reluctant but wanted to prevent Franco-Sardinian
                alliance.

1744   June 5. Frederick II concluded alliance with Louis XV of
                France. French to gain part of Belgium, Charles VII to
                conquer Bohemia after which Prussian army to advance
                against Vienna.

1745   Death of Emperor Charles VII ended war between Austria
                and Bavaria. Treaty formally signed at Fussen in April.

                June 5. Frederick won Battle of Hohenfriedberg but did
                not attempt move into Bohemia. Consequences of victory
                slight. Maria Theresa able to have her husband, Francis
                Stephen, elected Emperor over protest of Prussia and
                the Palatinate.

                August 26. Convention of Hanover concluded between
                Frederick and George II of England. Guaranteed each
                other's possessions, including Silesia for Prussia. Maria
                Theresa invited to adhere within six weeks, but refused.

                September 30. Frederick won Battle of Soor against
                overwhelming odds. Danger of Russian intervention
                dissipated. Maria Theresa tried to make peace with
                France so that she could concentrate on Frederick when
                latter suddenly offered to renew Treaty of Berlin.

                December 26. Peace of Dresden signed in which
                Prussia recognized election of Francis to Imperial
                throne, and Austria confirmed Prussia's cession of
                Silesia.

1746   Frederick II returned to Berlin where the people pro-
                claimed him "the Great" for first time. Soon Europe
                joined in this accolade.

1747   Johann Sebastian Bach welcomed to Potsdam by Frederick
                the Great.

1748   Peace of Aachen concluded by which Empress Maria
            Theresa achieved universal recognition of Pragmatic
            Sanction, losing only Silesia and small area in Italy.

1755   September. Austrians began to negotiate with France for
            potential alliance.

            December 7. Frederick II indicated willingness to
            arrange convention with England.

1756   January 16. Convention of Westminster concluded by
            which England and Prussia expressed desire to maintain
            peace in Germany and guaranteed its neutrality; agreed
            to oppose entrance into Germany or passage through it
            of any foreign army; and guaranteed each other's possess-
            ions. Beginning of "Diplomatic Revolution."

            May 1. First Treaty of Versailles concluded between
            Austria and France, defensive in nature.

            July 26. Frederick II had envoy at Vienna, Count Kling-
            grauffen ask Maria Theresa for explanation of move-
            ment of her armies. When not satisfied, Frederick
            issued ultimatum of August 20 demanding more explicit
            explanation and statement that she did not intend to attack
            him during the next year.

            August 29. Outbreak of Seven Years' War when Fred-
            erick II invaded Saxony. Frederick obtained possession
            of Saxony by October 20.

1757   January 11. Russia announced her adhesion to Treaty of
            Versailles as result of promises of compensation of
            Poland for territory taken by Prussia.

            February 2. Austro-Prussian Convention drawn up with
            exchange of ratification on May 19.

            May 1. New Treaty of Versailles signed in which France
            agreed to participate in war with more than 100,000 men
            and subsidies of 12 million livres.

            May 6. Austrians forced from their fortified positions
            before Prague and shut up in Bohemian capital by
            Prussia and her allies.

Summer. Russian army broke into East Prussia defeating a Prussian corps.

November 5. Frederick with 20,000 Prussians routed 50,000 French and Germans at Rossbach.

November 22. Austrians won victory which left them in possession of most of Silesia -- only temporary.

December 5. Frederick attacked Austrian army twice as strong at village of Leuthen west of Breslau.

1758

April 11. Prussia and England signed new treaty pledging themselves not to make separate peace. Prussia to receive 4 million thaler in annual subsidies and was free to choose her own military objectives.

May. Frederick chose Moravia as theater of operation. Had retreat in July.

August 25. Frederick's forces fought with Russians at Zorndorf. Found Russians more formidable than expected but able to force Russian retreat beyond Vistula for rest of year.

December 31. New Franco-Austrian Treaty in which French obligations were modified. Latter continued to pay large subsidies, but promised to aid in winning back Silesia.

1759

August 12. Frederick with 53,000 men attacked Russo-Austrian army of 70,000 at Kunersdorf and suffered most serious defeat of his life, losing one-half of army.

1760

April 1. Austro-Russian Treaty concluded promising Russians possession of East Prussia after war if Austria regained Silesia.

August 15. Frederick won victory at Liegnitz.

November 3. Frederick defeated Austrians in costly battle of Torgau.

1762

January 5. Death of Empress Elizabeth of Russia, succeeded by nephew Peter III. He was admirer of Frederick II and renounced all Russian conquests in Prussia and advised him to make peace.

May 5. Conclusion of war between Russia and Prussia.
Sweden followed suit.

June 19. Russo-Prussian alliance signed. Saved Prussia.

July 9. Deposition of imbecile Czar, was murdered on
July 19, and wife Catharine became Empress.

October 29. Frederick's brother, Prince Henry, defeated Empire Army at Freiberg in Saxony. Prussian
troops then went into Franconia and Thuringia. Frederick offered neutrality agreements which were accepted
by Bavaria, Wurttemberg, the Palatinate and Cologne.

November 3. Preliminaries of peace signed between
England and France at Fontainebleau giving England tre-
mendous gains, especially French withdrawal from North
America. Prussia neglected during negotiations. Rhenish possessions to be given to Austria to be used as pawns
in negotiations with Prussia. Frederick outraged.

1763   February 15. Treaty of Hubertusburg signed. Prussia
retained all her gains from first two Silesian wars.
Prussia could only expand with consent of Continental
powers.

October 5. August III died affording occasion for closer
relations between Russia and Prussia. Russia recognized Prussian acquisition of Silesia in return for which
Frederick had committed self to full cooperation in election of Catharine's candidate, Stanislaus Poniatowski, as
King of Poland, and to guarantee unworkable Polish constitution with liberum veto.

August 18. Emperor Francis died. Joseph considered
himself Emperor from that time. His mother, Maria
Theresa took him into joint rulership in December.

1764   April 11. Frederick and Catharine of Russia reaffirmed
their friendship by treaty to last eight years. Reciprocal
guarantee of their territories and agreement that neither
would arrange truce without other's consent.

1772   February 19. Prussia, Russia and Austria reached agreement on despoilation of Poland.

August 22. Treaty of Partition signed at St. Petersburg.

1776   Russian alliance, which was mainstay of Frederick's
        foreign policy during 1770's, prolonged until 1788.

1778   July 3. Frederick issued ultimatum declaring that
        Joseph II's convention with Charles Theodore, Elector
        Palatine, of January 3, did not give Austria any just
        claim to Lower Bavaria.

        July 5. Frederick crossed Bohemian frontier beginning
        War of Bavarian Succession.

        May 13. Frederick's willingness to grant Austria terri-
        torial concessions made Peace of Teschen possible.

1780   November 29. Maria Theresa died, leaving Joseph II as
        sole ruler of Austrian possessions.

1781   Immanuel Kant (1724-1804) published his Critique of Pure
        Reason which gained him European reputation.

        May. Arrangement between Austria and Russia. Both
        powers guaranteed each other's possessions. Russia
        promised Austria aid in case of Prussian attack.

        September. Austrian edict reduced criminal jurisdiction
        of lords, putting peasantry under protection of state.

1784   Kant's essay What is Enlightenment (Was 1st Aufklarung)
        published, defining Aufklarung as a coming of age.

1785   July 23. Prussia, Hanover and Saxony signed "Constitu-
        tional Association of Imperial Princes". Pledged to up-
        hold Constitution and institutions of Empire. Secret
        article bound them to oppose exchange or annexation of
        territories with arms.

1786   August 17. Frederick II died, succeeded by Frederick
        William II.

1788   Frederick William II intervened in internal affairs of the
        Netherlands because republicans had driven out his
        brother-in-law, William V of Orange. Prussian army
        under Duke Ferdinand of Brunswick brought Stadtholder
        back to the Hague.

1789   May 5. Louis XVI of France opened Estates General:
                beginning of first (peaceful) stage of French Revolution.

                July 14. Taking of Bastille in Paris, symbolic of struggle
                of lower classes against royal tyranny.

1790   February 20. Joseph II died, succeeded by Leopold II in
                Austria.

                July 27. Convention of Reichenbach signed. Leopold II
                promised to conclude Turkish War without acquisitions
                while Prussia ceased supporting revolutionary elements
                in various Habsburg lands.

                December 14. Leopold issued protest against Austrian
                decrees of French Assembly abolishing feudalism because
                it violated treaty rights of members of Empire who held
                lands in Alsace.

1791   Spring. Austria and Prussia agreed to recognize Poland's
                integrity and new constitution.

                May. Leopold II issued note to Monarchs of Europe, indi-
                cating that situation of French king was a matter of con-
                cern to other powers.

                September 21. Louis XVI accepted revised constitution
                and Leopold used this as excuse to take no further steps.

                August 27. Leopold II and Frederick William II met in
                Pillnitz, Saxony, rejecting demands of Count of Artois
                to aid emigré nobles. Austro-Prussian Declaration
                stated that events in France affected all sovereigns, and
                that Emperor and King would intervene to restore Louis
                XVI's freedom of action and introduce moderate constitu-
                tion.

                December 24. Leopold refused to disperse emigrés and
                complained of efforts of French to propagate sedition and
                discontent within Empire, especially Belgium.

1792   February 7. Austria and Prussia concluded a defensive
                alliance.

                March 1. Emperor Leopold died suddenly, succeeded by
                Francis II.

April 20. French legislature voted declaration of war against Francis II, followed in few days by declaration against Prussia.

July 1. Austria concluded treaty with Russia guaranteeing old constitution of Poland.

July 14. Last coronation of German Emperor took place in Frankfurt.

November 13. French troops won Battle of Brussels.

November 16. France declared Scheldt River open to commerce.

November 19. French decree promised fraternity and assistance to any nation engaged in recovering its liberty.

1793   January 21. Republican Party executed King Louis XVI of France.

April 30. France declared war on Empire.

September 23. Second Partition of Poland by Russia and Prussia in which Prussia received Danzig and large part of western Poland.

December 1. Lack of proper Austro-Prussian cooperation enabled Marshal Hoche to force Austrians from the Palatinate.

1794   March. Insurrection occurred at Cracow, culmination of national agitation in Poland.

April 17. Thaddeus Kosciuzsko, Polish patriot, expelled Russian garrison from Warsaw. Retook Vilna, August 22.

April 19. Prussia and England signed Treaty of the Hague by which latter to finance the war, but arrangement eventually broke down.

1795   April 5. Prussia and France signed Peace of Basel. French to occupy left bank of Rhine. Ultimate disposal of

territories to be arranged at final peace settlement.
Secret agreement: Prussia to have compensations east
of Rhine if Empire ceded left bank to France.

October 25. Third and final partition of Poland by
Austria, Prussia and Russia.

November 17. Catherine of Russia died. Czar Paul
favored Prussia.

December 21. Austrians concluded armistic with French.

1796   August 5. Franco-Prussian Treaty signed providing for
              compensation of first territory at expense of ecclesiasti-
              cal states.

1797   October 7. Peace of Campo Formio signed between Austria
              and France. Secret articles: France promised whole left
              bank of Rhine except Prussian territories.

              November. Frederick William II died, succeeded by son,
              Frederick William III.

1798   March. German Diet formally agreed to French possess-
              ion of Left Bank of the Rhine.

              August 10. Russo-German Convention concluded promis-
              ing military aid to Emperor.

1799   March 12. Austria declared war on France; Prussia
              only neutral state.

              October 22. After several bad defeats, Czar Paul
              announced secession from the Coalition, ordering
              Russian troops to start home in December.

1800   November 26. Austrians took offensive and crossed Inn
              River.

              December. Prussia adhered to League of Armed Neu-
              trality.

1801   February 9. Austria compelled by France to agree to
              Peace of Luneville, losing much territory on left bank of
              Rhine and leaving England isolated.

March. Denmark occupied Hamburg and Lubeck, on behalf of League of Armed Neutrality. Prussia then took
over Bremen, Hanover and Oldenberg to preserve neutrality of North Germany.

THE GERMANIC CONFEDERATION

1802   August 24. Deputation began work of planning for redis-
tribution of German territory after loss agreed to at
Luneville.

December 26. Treaty signed between Napoleon and
Emperor providing for peace and exchanges in territory.

1803.   February 25. German Diet drew up <u>Reichsdeputation-</u>
<u>shauptschluss,</u> "Final Recess," which drew many
boundaries existing well into 20th century.

April 27. Last of Imperial decrees was issued leading to
annihilation of 112 German states and creation of 33.

May. Peace of Amiens terminated and war began. Pitt
forged new continental alliance against Napoleon consisting of Russia, Sweden and Austria.

1804   August 14. Francis II assumed title and dignity of
hereditary emperor of Austria for all his dynastic
possessions.

September. Napoleon made tour of recent annexations
on left bank of Rhine.

October. Baron Heinrich Friedrich Karl vom und zum
Stein (1757-1831) became Prussian Minister of excise and
factory department of General Directory.

1805   October 21. Austrian army surrendered to Napoleon at
Ulm.

November 3. Frederick William signed Convention of
Potsdam by which Prussia to offer Napoleon certain
terms to be accepted within four weeks, otherwise
Prussia to join the Allies.

December 2. Austro-Russian army defeated at Battle of
Austerlitz.

December 6. Franco-Austrian armistice signed.

December 15. Treaty of Schonbrunn signed placing Prussia at Napoleon's disposal.

December 26. Austria signed Peace of Pressburg by which she had to accept and acknowledge constitutional and territorial changes made by Napoleon since Peace of Luneville.

1806   February 15. Franco-Prussian Treaty signed by Christian Haugwitz giving Prussia Hanover in return for which Prussia to bar Elbe and Weser to British ships.

April 5. England blockaded mouths of Elbe and Weser, seizing over 300 Prussian merchantmen and declaring war on Prussia on April 20.

July 12. Napoleon proposed establishment of Rhenish Confederation to be permanently allied to France.

August 1. Members of Confederation of the Rhine proclaimed secession from the Empire.

August 6. Emperor Francis laid down Crown of German Empire, simultaneously separating all his German lands from Empire.

October 9. Frederick William III issued war manifesto.

October 14. Napoleon won Battle of Jena defeating army of Prince Hohenlohe.

October 27. Napoleon arrived in Berlin forcing ministers and officials who remained behind to take oath to foreign conqueror.

November 21. Napoleon issued Berlin Decree excluding all British trade and Englishmen from Continent -- beginning of Continental system.

      Frederick William III decided against majority of his ministers and generals to continue war on side of Russia.

1807

January. Peace made between England and Prussia in which latter gave up claims to Hanover. England did not offer subsidies.

February 7 - 8. Battle of Eylau in Prussia: Napoleon failed to defeat Russian army under General Bennigsen. Prussian corps under Scharnhorst took substantial part in French setback.

April 26. Alexander I and Frederick William III concluded Treaty of Bartenstein to continue war until French were driven over the Rhine. English joined alliance on June 27.

July. Frederick William III made General Gerhard von Scharnhorst head of Commission for Military Reorganization. Commission recommended in 1808 introduction of universal service and creation of reserve militia.

July 7. Treaty of Tilsit signed between Russia and France. Czar Alexander convinced Napoleon to agree to survival of crippled Prussia.

July 9. Franco-Prussian Peace of Tilsit made even more oppressive by Convention of July 12. France to occupy Prussia west of the Elbe.

October 1. Baron Stein assumed office of principal civil minister. Served until November 24, 1808.

October 9. Royal Edict abolished three estates on which state rested.

December 1. France forced Prussia and other German states to break off relations with England and go to war against her.

Winter 1807 - 08. Johann Gottlieb Fichte delivered his Addresses to the German Nation in Berlin.

1808

Hegel to Nuremberg where he published his three volumes of Science of Logic (1812-1816).

Goethe's Faust appeared.

April. League of Virtue (Tugenbund) founded as instrument for creating anti-French feeling.

August 6. Prussian regulation concerning appointment of
ensigns published: knowledge and culture principles
for peacetime and bravery and intelligence in wartime.

November 19. Prussian Towns' Ordinance passed giving
control of most local affairs to towns.

1809   April 10. Austria, which had begun war on February 20,
delivered summons to whole German nationality to war
on France.

July 5 - 6. French attacked Austrians at Wagram, gaining costly but not wholly decisive victory.

August. Count Clemens Lothar Metternich (1773-1859)
headed government of Austria, remaining in power until
Revolutions of 1848.

1810   Firm of Krupp founded.

June 4. Hardenberg into power in Prussia.

1812   Jacob (1785-1863) and Wilhelm Grimm (1785-1859) published Fairy Tales for the Children and the Home.

February 24. Franco-Prussian Alliance signed in Paris.
Prussia to supply 20,000 men for Grande Armee.

March 11. Emancipation of Jews who adopted permanent
family names and accepted duty of military service.

May. Baron vom Stein began residence at Court of Czar
Alexander.

December 30. General Ludwig von Yorck, leader of
Prussian corps, signed convention with Russians pledging neutrality of his troops.

1813   January 21. Stein to Konigsberg to reinvigorate the
Germans.

February 27. Treaty of Kalisch: Prusso-Russian alliance concluded. Alexander to allow Prussia to have strip of Polish territory to provide easy connection between West Prussia and Silesia.

March 19. Russian-Prussian agreement providing Central Administrative Council for Germany with Stein at its head.

April. Scharnhorst created provincial militias consisting of all men not in the army or national guard in order to serve as home defense.

June 14. Prussia and England signed Treaty of Reichenbach in which two powers pledged selves to restore independence of states subdued by France.

October 14. Battle of Leipzig began: heaviest and bloodiest fighting between October 16 and 18. Napoleon lost one-third of army but allies failed to take advantage of situation.

1814

January 1. Allied armies invaded France, spearheaded by Prussian troops which crossed central Rhine; lack of unity in campaign.

February 3. Diplomatic Congress opened at Chatillon which negotiated with Napoleon until March 19, offering him frontiers of 1792.

March 1. Allies concluded Quadruple Alliance of Chaumont in which they pledged themselves to common pursuit of the war and avoidance of separate peace negotiations to be in force for 20 years.

March 31. Alexander I and Frederick William III made their entry into Paris with their guard troops. Louis XVIII became King of France.

May 30. First Peace of Paris negotiated with France by four major powers.

September 13. Frederick William signed law for universal military service making all Prussians from age of 20 to 39 liable to military service.

1815   January 3. Britain, Austria and France concluded a
                    secret alliance to fight together if attacked by Russia
                    and Prussia.

                    March 1. Napoleon returned from Elba, beginning of
                    the Hundred Days. His reappearance helped to reunify
                    the major powers.

                    May 22. Other German states promised constitutions
                    in order to stave off Prussian insistence on federal guar-
                    antee of constitutional principles, eventually compelled
                    Prussian government to issue constitution.

                    June 8. Federal Act of Germanic Confederation adopted
                    by German governments creating loose confederation of
                    35 monarchical states and four city republics.

                    June 12. Burschenschaft, new student organization,
                    founded in Jena under influence of Ludwig Jahn and histor-
                    ian Heinrich Luden to express the unity of Germany.

                    June 18. Battle of Waterloo: Napoleon's army completely
                    destroyed.

                    Summer. Lawyer Karl Hoffman formed German Society
                    in Nassau. Gneisenau and Hardenberg saw in League
                    useful tool to build up Prussian aims.

                    November 20. Second Treaty of Paris granting France
                    frontiers of 1790. France also had to pay moderate con-
                    tribution to allied powers.

1817   Hegel went from Heidelberg to Berlin under patronage of
                    Baron Altenstein, Prussian Minister of Education.
                    Taught men at University of Berlin who were to be on
                    almost every Faculty of learning in Germany except
                    Natural Science.

                    August. Hardenberg arranged for drafting of elementary
                    education law.

                    October 18. National Convention of Burschenschaften held
                    at Wartburg Castle on 300th anniversary of Luther's Re-
                    formation.

1818   May 26. Prussian Customs Law, work of Director-
General of Customs, Karl Georg Maasen, abolished all
internal duties, levied duties at external frontiers. Began
series of customs treaties. Prusso-German Zollverein
began operations January 1, 1834.

    September 28. Congress of powers at Aix-la-Chapelle:
Russia, Prussia, Austria and Great Britain. Reached
agreement on evacuation of France on October 1. Invited
French to join in deliberations on November 4 and signed
protocol on November 15 formally admitting France to
system of universal peace.

1819   Jacob Grimm published Deutsche Grammatik providing
grammarians with tools of analysis and instruction.

    March 23. Karl Ludwig Sand found in philosophy of
Karl Follen courage to assassinate playwright August
von Kotzebue (1761-1814). Latter was known to write re-
ports on German conditions for the Czar.

    April. In Frankfurt-am-Main, economist Friedrich
List (1789-1846) helped to found German trade and Industry Union to work for single frontier tariff for whole
of German Confederation.

    September 20. Reactionary Carlsbad Decrees rail-
roaded through Frankfurt Diet and became law October 1.

    October 18. King Frederick William commanded publi-
cation of Carlsbad Decrees in Prussia. Also approved
censorship edict which went far beyond German regulations, requiring that all printed matter be subjected to
censorship.

    October 25. First treaty of accession to Prussian
customs union signed by Prince of Sonderhausen.

1820   January 17. Prussian government issued ordinance concerning national debt indicating huge sums spent as result of Napoleonic period.

    May 30. Law issued regarding institution of taxation
which established foundation of fiscal system for generation.

October 20. Opening of Congress of Troppau, drew up protocol consecrating principle of intervention in states which had been or were undergoing revolutionary change of government.

1821   Peter Beuth founded Union for the Promotion of Industrial Zeal in Prussia.

January. Congress of powers reassembled at Laibach.

April 9. Military Constitution established German army of ten corps.

June 7. Promulgation of Prussian law dealing with partition of communal lands.

1822   October 20. Congress of Verona opened. Dealt with problem of Spanish Revolution. Metternich had submitted memorial condemning Spanish rebels. Conference closed December 14.

1823   January 6. Austria, Russia and Prussia delivered threatening notes to Madrid. French troops invaded Spain April 7.

December 11. Bundestag adopted resolution that in course of its proceedings, no appeal should be tolerated to new federal doctrines and theories.

1824   Leopold von Ranke published his first book Histories of the Latin and Germanic Nations from 1494-1514. Became professor at University of Berlin. Wanted to show history as it actually happened.

1825   October 12. King Max Joseph of Bavaria died, succeeded by son, Louis I, who transformed backward Munich into brilliant center of art and scholarship.

1828   February 14. Prussian-Hessian Trade Treaty signed setting pattern for constitution of German customs union.

April 26. Russia declared war on Turkey. Russia's poor showing led Metternich to try to get support against Russia. England agreed, but France and Prussia refused.

1830   July 27. Outbreak of French Revolution causing unrest
                in Germany.

                November 4. Convening of London conference of five
                powers: England, France, Austria, Prussia and Russia.
                Drew up Protocol December 20 agreeing to recognize
                Belgian independence. Agreed to Belgium's perpetual
                neutrality January 20, 1831.

1831   March 31. Rhine Navigation Convention into being.

                May 28. Danish King announced intention to introduce
                provincial diet modeled after Prussian into Schleswig
                and Holstein.

                June 29. Baron von Stein died.

1832   June 28. Germanic Confederation decreed strict limita-
                tions on authority of existing parliaments and on freedom
                of press.

1833   January 13. Metternich opened conference of German
                delegations at Vienna.

                March 9. Treaty of Berlin signed by Prussia, Russia and
                Austria pledging to settle Belgian issue by understanding
                with western powers.

                April 3. Frankfurt Putsch originated with groups of
                students' unions in hopes of starting general revolution
                in Germany by seizing guard house in Frankfurt. Plot
                failed miserably.

                June 12. German conference adopted final conservative
                protocol of 60 articles but did not publish them as Carls-
                bad decrees had been.

1834   January 1. Tariff Union established.

                March 6. Bundestag of German Federation demanded
                that Swiss government expel all Germans trying to dis-
                turb peace of German federal states after several Poles
                and Germans had invaded Savoy.

1840 June 7. Frederick William IV succeeded to Prussian throne on death of Frederick William III.

July 15. London Quadruple Alliance signed between four powers and Sultan of Turkey. Letter promised that Pasha would remain hereditary ruler of Egypt. Straits of Bosphorus and Dardanelles to be closed in peacetime to all nations.

September 7. Prussian Assembly approved memorial requesting king to complete and maintain constitutional system of representation founded by his father.

1841 July. After conversations with Austria, Frederick William IV agreed to extend federal laws regulating press and universities for six more years, although the king still wished to free the press.

December 24. Frederick William ordered provincial officials to be lenient in enforcement of censorship laws.

1842 May. Censorship upon illustrations abolished.

October 4. King granted right of free issue of all books in Prussia with more than 20 pages which was permissible under federal law.

1843 February 23. Ordinance issued in Prussia appointing local and district censors, entrusting enforcement to Supreme Court of censorship.

1844 June 28. Prussian Government published Ordinance Concerning Procedure in Questions Relating to Marriage which foreshadowed remodelling of entire marriage law.

1846 July 8. King Christian VIII of Denmark (1839-1848) issued "open letter" threatening to change legal status of German duchies of Schleswig and Holstein.

1847 February 3. Frederick William IV opened first session of the United Estates representing the various provinces of his kingdom.

1848 January 28. Frederick VII of Denmark proclaimed new Constitution uniting Duchies of Schleswig and Holstein more closely with Denmark.

February 24. Revolution broke out in Paris, France.
News set final spark to popular demonstrations for reform in Germany.

March 5   Fifty-one liberals met at Heidelberg and decided to summon preliminary assembly to make arrangements for election of National Assembly.

March 10. Diet at Frankfurt requested governments to
send men to help frame constitution.

March 13. Demonstrations began in Vienna. News
spread to Berlin by March 16 and tensions rose. Frederick William IV became convinced that concessions were
inevitable.

Metternich was removed from office as result of uprising.

March 19. Frederick William IV issued proclamation
to his "dear Berlin subjects" offering them forgiveness if
would put down barricades. Did not appease anyone.

March 21. Frederick William issued Declaration assuming role of leader in establishment of a United Germany.

March 31. Vorparlament or Preliminary Assembly met
at Frankfurt under Presidency of Professor Mittermaier
of Heidelberg, in active session until April 3 and nominal
session until May.

May 18. Frankfurt Parliament opened.

May 22. Prussian National Assembly convened to cooperate with government on Constitution.

August 12. Austrian Imperial Government decided to
open war against Hungarian revolution under leadership
of Louis Kossuth.

August 16 - 18. "The Association for the Protection of
the Interests of Landed Property" organized.

August 26. Following unsuccessful war with Denmark,
Prussia had to agree to inglorious armistice of Malmo.

October 19. Frankfurt Parliament began debate on draft
constituion.

October 22. Frankfurt Assembly passed constitutional
articles indicating its decision for grossdeutsch solution which would include Austria without its non-German
territories.

November 2. King Frederick William IV appointed
Count Frederick William Brandenburg Prime Minister.
Chief political inspiration of Cabinet was Minister of In-
terior, Baron Otto von Manteuffel.

November 12. State of siege declared all over Prussia
as part of plan to lead rebellion.

December. Struggle developed between pro-Austrian
Grossdeutsch and pro-Prussian Kleindeutsch forces.
Democrats believed that Greater Germany solution
would protect rights and privileges of man.

December 2. Archduke Francis Joseph ascended Austrian throne at age of 18. Was to rule until 1916.
Imbecile Emperor Ferdinand had been convinced to
resign.

December 5. Prussian Constitution imposed by King im-
pressed liberals, whereas many royalists found it to be
a surrender.

December 28. Constitution for Germany promulgated by
Frankfurt Parliament.

1849   March 28. Frankfurt Assembly chose Kleindeutsch solution and Frederick William IV emperor. Delegation
headed by its President, Eduard Simson, went to Berlin
April 3 to offer imperial throne to Prussian King. Frederick William refused crown.

April 28. General Joseph von Radowitz sent invitations
to German princes to appoint plenipotentiaries to meet in
Berlin to agree on new constitution based on one passed
at Frankfurt.

May 17. Series of conferences were held at Potsdam at
invitation of Prussian government. Conferees agreed to
work for eventual establishment of German Union.

May 14. Frederick William withdrew Prussian delegates from Frankfurt Assembly.

May 26. Close alliance signed by Kings of Prussia, Saxony and Hanover.

May 28. Constitution for German Union adopted at Potsdam.

July 10. Armistice arranged between Prussia and Denmark whereby Duchies of Schleswig and Holstein would remain occupied by Danes and Prussians.

July 23. Last fortress of German revolutionaries at Ratstatt capitulated. Among them was young Carl Schurz.

1850   January 31. Radowitz contributed substantially to the adoption of the Prussian Constitution.

March 20. National Assembly summoned by Frederick William IV met at Erfurt to consider Prussian leadership of German unification.

May 10. German princes met at Berlin, only twelve of whom were ready to accept a revised constitution for Germany without further changes.

April 26. Prince Schwarzenberg of Austria took initiative in opposing Prussian project of May 26, 1849, for union of German states. Race for favor of Czar began with Austria faring better because of Czar's attitude toward Schleswig-Holstein issue.

November 3. Count Brandenburg, seriously ill, died on November 6. Manteuffel became Prussian Prime Minister.

November 29. Manteuffel and Schwarzenberg of Austria signed an Austro-Prussian "punctuation" at Olmütz. Old order was restored in Holstein through Austrian and Prussian commissars acting for Germanic Confederation. Did not agree on common reform program to be presented at Dresden.

1851   July 15. Otto von Bismarck-Schonhausen was sent to Frankfurt as Prussian envoy.

1852   May 8. London Treaty arranged by the great powers
            recognizing Prince Christian of Glucksburg as heir to
            the Danish throne. Disturbances were settled in regard
            to Schleswig-Holstein, and Danish King Frederick VII
            proclaimed that the two duchies within the monarchy
            would receive their own administration.

1853   October 4. Turkey declared war on Russia -- opening
            of Crimean War. France and Britain eventually declared
            war on Russia, March 28, 1854.

1854   May 25. Beginning of meeting of Saxony, Bavaria and
            six other states signalizing existence of third Germany
            led by Max II of Bavaria, William of Wurttemberg and
            John of Saxony.

            April 20. Austro-Prussian Alliance allowed for protec-
            tion of German and non-German lands of Austria and
            Prussia.

            August 22. Austrian occupation of Rumanian Principali-
            ties began.

            December 22. Austria signed treaty with Napoleon III,
            guaranteeing former's Italian possessions.

1856   End of May. Czar Alexander II visited Frederick William
            IV in Berlin.

1858   October 7. Frederick William IV suffered number of
            strokes in 1857 which had incapacitated him. Brother
            William became regent.

1859   March 3. Secret Franco-Russian alliance signed con-
            taining specific promise by Russia of her benevolent neu-
            trality in event of Franco-Austrian war in Italy. Russia
            willing to accept French acquisition of Savoy.

            April 22. Outbreak of Italian War supported by Napoleon
            III of France, who declared war on May 3. Greatly
            alarmed leaders and public opinion of Germany.

            June 4. Franco-Italian victory of Magenta defeating
            Austria in which latter was forced to recognize role that
            Prussia deserved in German and European affairs.

August 14. Great meeting at Eisenach by democratic leaders, issued Declaration calling on all Germans to defend national independence.

July 11. Peace of Villafranca which Napoleon III rushed to conclude in order to avoid possibility of Prussia's entrance into the war.

September 15 - 16. National Union (Nationalverein) founded as result of Italian events and chiefly by initiatives of northwestern and southwestern liberals and democrats to awaken all people to urgency of German national unification. Democrats now accepted kleindeutsch solution.

1859   December. General Albrecht von Roon (1803-1879) appointed Minister of War. Reform of army was central objective of regent's policy.

1860   February 10. Army Bill proposed to increase size, strength and efficiency of army. Aim of Roon's reform was novel system of active and reserve service. Majority of generals thought two-year service was sufficient but felt had to accede to Prince Regent's wishes in regard to three-year service.

1861   January 2. William acceded to throne after death of his brother.

BISMARCK AND THE GERMAN EMPIRE

1862   May 22. Bismarck named Ambassador to Paris.

August 2. Negotiations between Paris and Berlin led to agreement including provisions for free exchange of goods and adoption of most-favored-nation clause.

September 22. Otto von Bismarck met William I who was ready to abdicate. Bismarck declared his readiness to defend the army bill and royal supremacy even against hostile parliament.

September 23. Large majority in Parliament refused to pass first financial measures for William's army. Majority of cabinet recommended compromise but William I stood firm.

September 30. Bismarck as Chancellor delivered
famous "Blood and Iron" speech.

1863   January 22. Serious national revolts occurred in Russian
Poland. Bismarck feared that it would spread to Poles in
Prussia.

February 8. General Gustav von Alvensleben signed Convention between Prussia and Russia. Each nation would
supply troops to help the other in case insurgents threatened them.

April 18. Prussian Landtag passed Commercial Treaty
with Belgium which had been signed March 28.

June 1. Bismarck issued ordinance imposing drastic restrictions on freedom of the press.

August 16. Emperor of Austria opened assembly of
German Princes at Frankfurt to discuss reform of Confederation. Bismarck persuaded King William to refuse
invitation, and Prussia rejected reform on September 22.

November 13. Danish Parliament passed new Constitution
incorporating Schleswig into Danish Kingdom. Frederick
VII died November 15, successor Christian IX accepted
new constitution on November 20, violating London Treaty
of 1852.

1864   January 16. Austrian and Prussian governments presented
ultimatum in Copenhagen demanding cancellation of Constitution of November 1863. Danish government rejected,
and Austria and Prussia declared war.

April 25 - June 25. London Conference. Bismarck proposed personal union of duchies and separation from Denmark. When conference adjourned Austria and Prussia
at liberty to settle conflict by themselves.

August 1. Preliminary peace signed between Denmark and
German states, later codified in Vienna Peace Treaty of
October 30. Austria and Prussia received Schleswig-
Holstein.

August 20-24. Conversations held at Schönbrunn between
Austrian and Prussian monarchs, as well as Bismarck
and Austrian Foreign Minister, Count Johann von Rechberg.

Proposed Prussian support for reconquest of Austria's position in North and Central Italy in return for which Austria to give Schleswig-Holstein to Prussia and respect latter's predominance in North Germany.

December 8. Pope Piux IX issued Encyclical Quanta Cura with its Syllabus denouncing practically all liberal principles, thereby arousing anger of European liberals.

1865   February 22. Bismarck announced conditions under which Prussia would be willing to agree to creation of duchy of Schleswig-Holstein under Augustenberg prince within Germanic Confederation. Austria rejected.

August 14. Gastein Convention signed. Prussia retained her sovereign rights in both duchies. Prussia agreed only to factual separation of joint administration, but Convention made it possible at any moment to reopen all political issues.

December 31. Italian Trade Treaty made with Zollverein.

1866   January 26. Bismarck accused Austrians of breach of Gastein Convention because they tolerated renewed popular agitation for Duke of Augustenburg.

April 8. Prusso-Italian Alliance signed. Italy promised to go to war if Prussia would go to war against Austria within three months.

June 1. Austria requested Diet of Germanic Confederation to intervene in Schleswig-Holstein dispute. Bismarck accused Austria of violating Treaty of Alliance of January 14, 1864, as well as Gastein Convention.

June 2. William I authorized Helmuth von Moltke to issue orders in his name to all the army commanders, bypassing Minister of War.

June 9. General Edwin von Manteuffel led Prussian troops from Schleswig into Holstein.

June 10. Bismarck presented plan for formation of new German Constitution in event of collapse of Germanic Confederation.

June 12. Austria concluded secret treaty with France in
which she promised to cede Venetia after victorious war
in Germany. Napoleon III hoped to use this agreement as
a protective device for insuring the chance of French intervention.

1866

June 14. Bavaria moved in Federal Diet for mobilization
of all non-Prussian and non-Austrian forces. Prussian
representative declared Federal Act broken and conse-
quently void.

June 24. War broke out.

July 3. Austrians defeated at Battle of Sadowa. Found
they could not rely on other states.

Elections held for Prussian Parliament. Liberals reduced in number of seats and conservatives vastly increased.

July 5. Austria ceded Venetia to Napoleon III at his request. Bismarck was forced to negotiate with French
government.

July 26. Bismarck reached agreement with Austria on
preliminary peace. Austria withdrew from Germany pay-
ing only small war indemnity but making no territorial
concessions.

August 13 - 22. Bismarck concluded treaties of alliance
with Wurttemberg, Baden and Bavaria -- all guaranteeing
each other's integrity and promised to place all their
military forces under Prussian command should there be
war against foreign power.

August 18. Prussia concluded treaty of federation with
North German States.

August 23. Final Peace Treaty signed with Austria in
Prague. One article stipulated international independence of future South German Confederation, considered
unrealistic and obnoxious by Bismarck.

September 3. Prussian Parliament voted indemnity bill
whereby Parliament granted indemnity for having conducted to its administration without a budget.

1867   April 3. Bismarck advised King William III of the Nether-
            lands not to sell Luxembourg to France, warning that it
            might lead to war.

            April 16. Constitution of North German Confederation
            enacted. Elections for Reichstag took place in May.

1868   August Bebel (1840-1913) and Wilhelm Liebknecht (1826-
            1900) induced a workers' convention in Nuremberg to
            adopt a declaration in favor of International Workingmen's
            Association.

1869   Full emancipation and restoration of former legal status
            granted to Jews in North Germany. Granted to all Ger-
            many after 1871.

            Law of North German Confederation gave workers legal
            right to organize.

1870   February. First official contacts between Spanish gov-
            ernment of Marshal Prim, which was searching for suit-
            able candidate for Spanish throne, and Prince Leopold of
            Hohenzollern-Sigmaringen. Bismarck encouraged King
            William to favor the project after initial refusal, and
            Spaniards approached Leopold again in June.

            June 19. Prince Leopold accepted Spanish throne offer.

            July 2. Spanish Cabinet announced candidacy of Prince
            Leopold. French government suspected Prussian plot.

            July 5. Duke of Gramont, French foreign minister, ex-
            pressed opposition of France to German prince on
            Spanish throne.

            July 9 - 13. Several meetings between King William I
            and French Ambassador, Count Benedetti, at Ems.
            William indicated would not object if Prince Leopold
            changed his mind voluntarily. Occurred when Karl
            Anton informed Paris and Madrid of son's resignation on
            July 12. French government tried to exploit Prussian re-
            treat by instructing Benedetti to request William to issue
            statement approving of Leopold's resignation but also
            that he would not tolerate any future candidacy of the
            Prince. Bismarck received report by telegram. Was
            given permission to give information to the press and Ger-
            man diplomats. Edited despatch made it appear that King
            refused to see Benedetti.

July 18. Vatican Council announced dogma of infallibility.
Pope's primacy over bishops was affirmed and his ex
cathedra decisions in matters of faith and morals was
declared infallible.

July 19. France declared war against Prussia and North
German Confederation.

September 1. General von Moltke able to force Marshal
MacMahon to accept battle at Sedan. MacMahon and Emperor Napoleon III surrendered on September 2.

September 4. Republican "Government of National Defense" formed in Paris under General Trochu along with
Leon Gambetta and Jules Favre. Rejected any concessions to Germans.

November 9. Russian Government renounced clause of
Peace of Paris of 1856 which forbade Russia from maintaining naval forces on Black Sea.

1871   January 18. On 170th anniversary of coronation of first
Prussian king, William I was proclaimed Emperor of
Germany in Hall of Mirrors of Versailles Palace.

May 4. Constitution of German Empire adopted.

May 10. Germany and France signed Peace Treaty.

July 8. Bismarck dissolved "Catholic Section" of
Prussian Ministry of Ecclesiastical Affairs and Education, believing was tool of Church within Prussian government.

December. The 33 state currencies were abolished to
be replaced by German mark. French war indemnity
facilitated transition making it possible to base new
currency on gold.

1872   January 22. Adelbert Falk appointed Prussian minister
of Religious Affairs.

March 8. Order abolished supervision of schools by
churches. Meant acceptance of program by state schools.

October 6 - 7. Economist Lujo Brentano (1844-1931) convened conference of scholars interested in social problems
at Eisenach. Founded Association for social policy hop-
ing to encourage some form of governmental regulation
of social problems.

1873   Wilhelm Marr published The Victory of Judaism over
              Teutonism in which he introduced term, anti-semitism,
              charging that Jews were responsible for destruction of
              healthy economy.

              January 9. Minister of Religious Affairs Falk introduced
              laws concerning Catholic Church, passed on May 15.
              Priests and Ministers had to study under German educa-
              tional system. Aim of "May Laws" was to minimize all
              training by church schools; beginning of Kulturkampf.

              May 4. "Expatriation Law" passed giving government
              power to confine or even ban from Empire those clerics
              who practice their priestly functions without approval of
              state.

1874   March 9. Civil marriage made compulsory as part of
              Bismarck's campaign to reduce power and influence of
              Church.

1875   February 5. Papal Encyclical declared whole ecclesi-
              astical legislation of Prussia invalid, threatening those
              who obey it with ex-communication. Prussian law of
              April 22 stopped all financial support of the Church.

              March. Bismarck published decree forbidding export of
              horses from Germany because he was informed that
              French had been purchasing thousands of horses for their
              cavalry.

              April 5. Kölnische Zeitung published article calling re-
              organization of the French army preparation for war.

              May 1. War scare developed because of French Assembly's
              passage of law increasing size of army in case of war. Bri-
              tish offered their diplomatic help in Franco-German differ-
              ences

May 18. Russian Emperor and Minister Gortchakoff
arrived in Berlin. Told William I and Bismarck that
Europe would not stand by if war broke out between
France and Germany.

1876   August. Richard Wagner's <u>Ring of the Nibelungen</u> initially
performed at first Bayreuth festival. Had begun work in
1848.

1877   April 24. Russo-Turkish War broke out.

June. Anti-Socialist laws passed.

1878   February 22. Bismarck began movement which eventually led to ending of Kulturkampf.

May 11. Vain attempt made on life of William I. Although
had no connection with Social Democratic Party, Bismarck
presented law banning the party to the Reichstag.

June 13 - July 13. First International Congress held in
Berlin to settle issues remaining after Russo-Turkish
War; evidence of Germany's eminent position among
nations.

October 21. Anti-Socialist Law passed under which all
Social Democratic, Socialist and Communist associations, meetings and publications could be forbidden or
dissolved. Achieved complete destruction of existing
Social Democratic Party institutions.

December 15. First official declaration by Government
for protection of industries was issued.

1879   June 12. Reichstag passed tariff laws.

October 7. Austro-German Alliance signed -- lasted
until 1918. Alliance was for Bismarck the most important
instrument for making Central Europe secure against
Russian inroads, as well as serving to strengthen Germany against France. Bismarck still continued to believe that something had to be done to improve relations
with Russia.

1881   League of German Students (Verein Deutscher Studenten)
                founded to propagate anti-semitism and nationalism in
                German universities.

                June 18. Three Emperors' Alliance formally signed
                (Austria-Hungary, Germany and Russia). Three powers
                pledged selves to maintain benevolent neutrality if one
                of them was at war with fourth power. Real problem was
                friction of Austria and Russia over Balkans.

                June 28. Austria-Hungary concluded alliance with Serbia
                making former protector of the principality.

1882   May 20. Triple Alliance concluded (Italy, Austria-Hun-
                gary, and Germany). Was defensive alliance against'
                France. Was strengthening of political and social order
                through monarchical principle.

1883   June 15. Law introduced health insurance for large seg-
                ment of wage earners.

1884   July 6. Law on accident insurance passed with whole
                cost underwritten by employers. Took over losses after
                14th week.

                April 24. Bismarck declared German protectorate over
                what became German South-west Africa.

                October 15. Germany proclaimed her sovereignty over
                Togoland and the Cameroons.

                November - February 1885. West Africa Conference met
                at Berlin. All powers recognized the International Associ-
                ation of the Congo which Bismarck named the Congo Free
                State. Some limitations to British monopoly in colonial
                realm were developed.

1885   February 27. William I granted Society for German
                Colonization, formed in 1884, a charter of protection.
                Gave it rights in territory it controlled in Africa -- be-
                ginning of German East Africa Company.

                May 5. Edict expelled all Poles who were not Prussian
                subjects from Prussian Poland. Led to passage of Coloni-
                zation Law for Polish districts in 1886: largely a failure.

Eventually led to creation of "Association for the Advancement of the German Nationality in Eastern Marches" in 1894.

1887   February 20. Bismarck renewed Triple Alliance.

June 18. Reinsurance Treaty signed in Berlin with Russia. Two countries promised each other benevolent neutrality in case one were at war with third power, even if Russia or Germany were to start war against Austria-Hungary or France. Both powers agreed not to tolerate changes in Balkans without prior assent. Treaty intended to thwart possible Franco-Russian alliance.

December 12. As result of Bismarck's moral encouragement, Lord Salisbury transformed Mediterranean Entente, signed between England and Italy to maintain status quo in Mediterranean on February 12, 1887, into Triple Alliance which guaranteed integrity and independence of Turkish Empire as well as Turkish control of the Dardanelles.

1888   March 9. William I died at age of 91. His son, Emperor Frederick III was dying of cancer of the throat. Bismarck remained in control of the government.

June 15. Frederick III died. William II succeeded his father to the throne.

October 4. The Deutsche Bank, headed by Georg von Siemens, received concession along with other German businessmen from Turkish government for building railroad from Constantinople to Ankara.

1889   January. Bismarck cautiously explored possibility of secret or public alliance with England for joint defense against French aggression.

April 20. Adolph Hitler born in Braunau-on-the-Inn, Austria.

May. As result of strike of miners in Ruhr District, William II decided show monarchical benevolence toward workers. Program proposed, enacted 1891, abolishing Sunday work and limiting working hours of women and children.

May 18. Law on old age and disability insurance passed.

June 22. Pension insurance enacted.

1890   Colonial League founded by Carl Peters.

January 25. Reichstag rejected bill to renew anti-Socialist legislation.

February 20. Elections were held. Resentment against Bismarck's policy welled up.

THE ERA OF WILLIAM II

March 18. Otto von Bismarck was dismissed. Count Leo Caprivi was made Chancellor and Prussian Prime Minister.

July 1. Anglo-German agreement giving Heligoland to Germany but ceding German claims on Zanzibar and Witu to Great Britain signed.

July 29. Act set up arbitration courts to deal with disputes between employer and employee.

1891   January. Count Alfred von Schlieffen (1833-1913) appointed Chief of Staff.

Pan-German League founded by Alfred Hugenberg for the cultivation of German national ideals. Eventually merged with the Colonial League.

June. Issuance of Emperor's Arbeiterschutzgesetz: was complicated and comprehensive code of labor regulations.

December 18. Reichstag passed trade treaties arranged with Austria, Italy, Switzerland and Belgium.

1892   Friedrich Nietzsche (1844-1900) published Thus Spake Zarathustra was meant to be invitation to think of individual constantly working to transcend himself, but interpreted as endorsement of political program.

First general Congress of German Trade Unions held at Halberstadt; basis for building trade unions along organizational lines.

1893   February. Federation of Agriculturists (<u>Bund</u> <u>der</u> <u>Land-</u><u>wirte</u>) founded. Aim was to get protection and support from government through tariffs, credits and low taxes.

1894   May 12. France and Germany forced Britain to withdraw from treaty with Congo State by which she would have been able to build   Cape to Cairo Railroad as exclusive British enterprise.

            August 1. Outbreak of Sino-Japanese War: complete defeat of China by 1895 led William II's government to realize necessity of securing naval station and therefore, cooperating with Russia.

            October 29. William II dismissed Caprivi because of storm against some of his policies and appointed Prince Chlodwig Hohenlohe German Chancellor and Prussian Prime Minister.

            December. Franco-Russian Military Convention signed.

1895   Experiments of Wilhelm Roentgen (1845-1923) led to discovery of the X-ray.

            Opening of Kiel Canal connecting Baltic and North Seas.

            May 5. Germany and France forced Japan to retrocede her conquests to China.

1896   January 3. William II dispatched telegram to President Paul Kruger of Transvall congratulating him on putting down Dr. Jameson's raid without appealing to friendly foreign powers.

            November. Friedrich Naumann pastor in Evangelical Church created National Social Union, aiming to familiarize Left Liberals with ideas of Max Weber.

1897   Count Alfred von Schlieffen, Prussian Chief-of-Staff from 1891-1906, drafted first complete plan of operation against France. Reached its classic form in plan of 1905.

            June. Count Bernhard von Bulow became foreign secretary.

June 17. William II appointed Admiral Alfred von Tirpitz head of the Admiralty with assignment to build great navy.

November 14. Germany used pretext of murder of two German missionaries to gain 90-year concession of Kiachow territory on Shantung Peninsula from China.

1898   Germany bought Caroline and Mariana Islands in Pacific from Spain.

Eduard Bernstein published The Presuppositions of Social-ism and the Tasks of Social Democracy in which he denied validity of Marx's theory of impoverishment of the proletariat and the approaching final crisis of capital-ism.

German Navy League founded at instigation of Admiral von Tirpitz as propaganda agent for building good navy.

March. Joseph Chamberlain approached German Ambass-ador in London with suggestion of Anglo-German Alli-ance. Received with suspicion and never concluded. Germany did remain strictly neutral when Boer War be-gan in October 1899.

August 20. Germany and Britain signed agreement about Portugese colonies to grant Portugal a loan to extricate her from her financial difficulties.

November 29. Sultan of Turkey granted German Anatol-ian Railway Company preliminary concession for railway to Bagdad and Borsa.

1900   Max Planck published the first version of his quantum theory.

January 1. Civil Code went into effect for Germany.

October 17. Count Bernhard von Bulow replaced Hohen-lohe as Chancellor.

1902   Anglo-Japanese Alliance concluded as Britain began to remove herself from state of isolation.

December 14. Agricultural Protection Act passed.

1903   March. Elaborate Child Labor Law passed.

1904   England turned to building new type of battleship, the
              Dreadnought, more heavily armored and armed than
              existing battleships. Germany was able to produce its
              own first modern battleship by 1907.

              April 8. England and France reached settlement of all
              their colonial conflicts.

1905   Albert Einstein presented his special theory of relativity.

              March 31. William II landed at Tangiers for visit to
              show support for Sultan of Morocco.

              Summer. William II met his cousin, Czar Nicholas II,
              in Bjoerkoe on Finnish Coast with no official Russian or
              German minister in attendance. William lured Czar into
              signing Russo-German Alliance, criticized by ministers.

              July. French government agreed to conference at Al-
              geciras, Spain near Gibraltar to be held in January 1906,
              to discuss issues involving Morocco. British support
              of France's position at conference indicated strength
              of Anglo-French Entente. Germany's international situ-
              ation became very precarious.

1906   Helmuth von Moltke, nephew of elder Moltke, became
              Schlieffen's successor, still maintaining Schlieffen Plan.

1907   Friedrich Meinecke published his Cosmopolitanism and
              National State containing studies on origin of German
              nation.

              Fall. Hitler went to Vienna for first time to try to
              enter Academy of Fine Arts as architecture student,
              but did not pass entrance examination.

              December 21. Hitler's mother died. He returned to
              Vienna in February 1908 to resume his life as an artist.

1908   October 6. Turkish Revolution caused renewal of vari-
              ous and conflicting aspirations on Balkan Peninsula.
              Bulgaria won her independence from Turkey.

October 7. Austria declared annexation of Bosnia and Herzegovinia which was blow to Serbia's protector, Russia.

October 28. London Daily Telegraph published interview with William II in which he posed as staunch friend of England claiming that he had given the British staff the war plan that enabled the army to bring the Boer War to successful conclusion. Some questioned stability of William II.

1909   July 14. Von Bulow resigned as Chancellor leaving the problem of naval competition to his successor Theobald von Bethmann-Hollweg (1856-1921).

1911   Italy declared war against Turkey over Tripolitania setting stage for war of Serbia, Bulgaria and Greece against Turkey which broke out in Spring of 1912.

April. French sent troops to Fez, capital of Morocco. German gunboat, the Panther, was sent to West Morocco to put pressure behind German demands that its interests in Morocco be protected in Morocco, and that France cede parts of French Congo to Germany.

October. Settlement reached between France and Germany over Morocco. France to cede some Congo territory to Germany.

1912   February. Lord Haldane, British Secretary of War, went to Berlin to reach agreement on naval armaments and general political understanding.

British reached agreement with French under which former would protect Channel area and Atlantic coast, and French would base their fleet in the Mediterranean.

1913   National Convention of Wandervogel met at Hohe Meissner Mountain. Members dedicated themselves to better life to be shaped on their own initiative.

1914   June 28. Gavrilo Princip, a student, who was a Serbian by race and Austro-Hungarian by nationality, killed Archduke Francis Ferdinand of Austria and his wife at Sarajevo, capital of Bosnia. Austrians suspected Serbian government was somewhat involved although had no direct evidence.

July 7. German "blank check" issued tipping scales in Austro-Hungarian cabinet to war party.

July 20 - 23. French President, Poincaré, and Premier Viviani were on state visit to Russia.

July 23. Presentation of Austro-Hungarian ultimatum in Belgrade with time limit for reply of 48 hours was made.

July 25. Serbia's reply to Austro-Hungarian ultimatum went far in accepting Austrian demands except those which infringed on Serbian sovereignty. As a result, she mobilized her army.

July 28. Habsburg monarchy declared war on Serbia.

July 29. Russians announced partial mobilization of army as answer to Austrian mobilization against Serbia. General von Moltke gave German Chancellor strong and detailed warning against the inescapable automatism of this mobilization.

July 30. Prince Lichnowsky, German Ambassador in London, relayed Earl Grey's repeated proposal of 4-power mediation as well as German-British mediation in Vienna, St. Petersburg and Belgrade. Austria-Hungary refused this offer.

July 31. Declaration of war against Russia prepared -- to be delivered at 5 P.M. by German Ambassador to St. Petersburg.

August 1. Difficulties involved in sticking to Schlieffen Plan revealed. Britain seemed to suggest that it would stay neutral if Germany would desist from westward drive.

August 2. Germany concluded alliance with Turkey and Turkey joined in war in October.

        Labor unions agreed to avoid impeding war effort if government promised not to take any repressive action against unions.

August 4. William II addressed <u>Reichstag</u> concerning the war.

Germany invaded Belgium galvanizing British liberal opinion in favor of the war against Germany.

August 23. Colonel-General Paul von Hindenburg (1847-1934) called into service from retirment, assuming command of German forces along Russian front. Colonel Erich Ludendorff (1854-1937) was appointed his Chief of Staff.

Japan declared war on Germany.

September 4 - 15. Battle of the Marne: German military writers took view that Battle was lost because of Moltke's fumbling, but Schlieffen Plan could never really have achieved full success.

September 14. General von Moltke replaced as Chief of Staff by General Erich von Falkenhayn.

October 17 - 30. Battle of the Yser. Belgians opened dikes and flooded large sections of coastal region when German victory was at hand.

November 3. England declared whole North Sea a war zone, interfering with navigation of neutral nations.

December. Allies began winter battle of Champagne.

December 3. Germany lost five ships at Battle of Falkland Islands basically driven from seas.

1915   February. Gallipoli expedition started as combined Anglo-French enterprise with naval bombardments. Troops landed in April but close coordination not followed.

February 4. Germany announced that within two weeks she would begin to engage in unlimited submarine warfare. She fixed war zone in which ships would be destroyed on sight.

February 7 - 27. Winter battle of Masurian Lakes won by German soldiers even more against climate than against enemy.

April 26. Secret Treaty of London in which Allied Powers paid extraordinary price to gain Italy's entry into the war.

May 7. British liner, Lusitania, sunk with loss of 1,200 lives including 139 Americans. This caused outbreak of popular anti-German feeling in America.

September 6. Alliance concluded between Central Powers and Bulgaria which then declared war on Russia in October.

September 25. French and British resumed their Spring offensives in the Champagne and the Artois on much larger scale.

End September. All of Poland, Lithuania, as well as half of Latvia conquered.

October 6. Campaign against Serbians begun.

1916
February 21. Germans unleashed attack on Verdun. Early German successes caused temporary crisis in French defense.

March 25. Sinking of unarmed French Channel boat, Sussex, resulted in loss of 80 lives, including many Americans. Evoked American ultimatum to stop unrestricted submarine warfare. Germans agreed on condition that they had the right to renew it whenever they thought it would be necessary.

May 31. Only major naval engagement of war took place off Jutland. Two navies locked in battle in which German fleet displayed better armor and gunnery, and British lost twice as much tonnage. Yet German fleet could not prevail.

August 27. Rumania declared war on Austria-Hungary.

August 29. Field Marshal von Hindenburg appointed Head of Supreme Command. Erich Ludendorff was named his Chief-of-Staff with rank of First Quartermaster General.

November 21. Emperor Francis Joseph died. New Emperor Charles was convinced that Austria-Hungary was unable to fight much longer. He explored possibilities of peace.

December 12. German government decided to take initiative as peacemaker. Issued invitation for opening of peace negotiations.

December 18. President Woodrow Wilson of the United States issued his call to all belligerents to state their war and peace aims.

1917   January 9. German leaders reached fateful decision to reopen unrestricted submarine warfare on February 1.

January 19. German Foreign Minister, Arthur Zimmerman, sent telegram to Ambassador in Mexico, informing him of imminent renewal of unlimited submarine warfare, the hope of keeping United States neutral, and if the United States should go to war, desire to bring Mexico in as Germany's ally. Note intercepted by British and turned over to American Ambassador, Walter Hines Page.

January 31. German government, prodded by President Wilson, gave toned-down version of its peace program, also informed him of renewal of unrestricted submarine warfare on February 1.

February 3. United States broke off diplomatic relations with Germany.

April 6. United States declared war on Germany.

April 7. William II's "Easter Message" promised Prussian people universal and direct, but not equal suffrage.

July 6. Matthias Erzberger, Reichstag deputy, began agitation for assembly to assume greater control of governmental affairs and develop policy of peace negotiations.

July 13. Bethmann-Hollweg retired as Chancellor. Replaced by George Michaelis (1857-1936), a career interior official who had approval of the Generals.

August 1. Pope Benedict V delivered peace overture (presented in Berlin August 15). Pope proposed disarmament, mutual renunciation of territory and war indemnities, freedom of the seas, and establishment of international court of arbitration.

October 9. Chancellor Michaelis opened attack against Independent Socialist Party. Ebert demanded resignation of Chancellor. As tensions increased, and indirect and unofficial vote of no-confidence by the majority led to Michaelis' downfall. Was replaced by Count Hertling on November 1.

November 7 - 8. Kerensky government overthrown by Bolsheviks in Russia.

December 20. Representatives of Central Powers met Russian delegation at fortress town of Brest-Litovsk.

1918   January 18. President Wilson delivered his Fourteen Point speech. Count Hertling, German Chancellor, disparaged Wilsonian Program in speech before Reichstag on January 24.

Russians returned to Brest-Litovsk where Trotsky prolonged the negotiations by speeches aimed at arousing masses in the capitalist countries.

January 28. Great strike of 400,000 workers began in Berlin and spread to many cities. Strikers demanded more food, speedy peace arrangements without annexations, as well as democratization of German political institutions.

February 18. German troops began their eastward and northeastward drive, meeting practically no resistance. As a result, they occupied Kiev on March 1.

March 3. Bolsheviks signed dictated peace of Brest-Litovsk.

March 7. Munich locksmith, Anton Drexler, set up Committee of Independent Workmen.

Group of German-Finnish treaties signed in Berlin. Finns promised not to conclude any foreign alliances without German agreement nor to tolerate any foreign military bases except German naval bases.

March 21. First German offensive launched in West, failed by end of March.

May 7. German Government forced Rumania to sign Peace Treaty of Bucharest.

May 27. Second German offensive opened; stopped by mid-July.

June - August. Various mutinies occurred in Navy.

July 18. Second Battle of Marne was the turning point of the war. Offensive strength of German army was broken.

August 8. Strong allied offensive mounted at the Somme taking Germans by surprise.

September 14. Austro-Hungarian government made bid for peace negotiations turned down by the Allies.

September 30. Armistice arrangements completed with Bulgaria.

October. Thomas Mann published Meditations of a Non-Political Man.

October 3. Prince Max of Baden (1867-1929) took office as Chancellor.

October 13 - 14. Hitler's eyes affected by gas attack at western front.

October 18. Anton Drexler and Karl Harer founded Political Workers' Circle.

October 28. New constitutional order was perfected with law amending Bismarckian constitution going into force.

October 29. William II went to spa to plan move against government.

Navy revolted.

October 30. Turks signed armistice with Allied Powers.

November 4. Uprising at Kiel demanded liberation of
600 sailors imprisoned for naval uprising.

November 5. American government informed Germans
that Allied Powers were willing to grant an armistice.

November 7. Revolution took place in Munich prompted
by desire for peace.

November 9. Prince Max of Baden prematurely announced
abdication of the Emperor. William finally agreed and
at 5 A.M. on November 10, his train left for Holland.

   Philip Scheidenmann, Social Democrat Deputy, proclaimed Republic from outer steps of <u>Reichstag</u> building.

November 11. At 5 A.M. Matthias Erzberger, chief
delegate of Armistice Negotiations Committee signed
armistice. Guns all along the lines became silent at
11 A.M.

December 4. Proclamation of Spartacists by Rosa Luxemburg condemning Hohenzollerns as agents of imperial-
istic bourgeoisie and Junkers and claiming that bourgeois
class rule was guilty of the World War.

December 23. Uprising of 1,000 sailors who came to
Berlin after Revolution. Demanded payment of large sum
of money by the government. On December 24, troops
attacked palace and stables.

December 30. Spartacus League held convention and
reconstituted self as Communist Party.

                   THE WEIMAR REPUBLIC

1919   January. Allied statesmen assembled at Versailles for
              Peace conference.

              German Workers' Party founded by Harrer and Drexler.

              January 6. Government Printing office and Silesian rail-
              road station into Spartacist hands. Gustav Norske with
              aid of old army and Freikorps freed Berlin between Janu-
              ary 11 and 15.

January 19. Elections for Constituent National Assembly took place with no disturbance.

February 3. German Council of Workers' and Soldiers' Soviets handed over its powers to National Constituent Assembly.

February 6. National Assembly convened in Weimar's national theater. Elected Friedrich Ebert president.

February 13. Philip Scheidemann formed government.

March 3. Workers' Councils of Berlin proclaimed general strike as demonstration for socialization. Communists used occasion for armed uprising.

April 7. Communist Republic installed in Munich. Defeated by Bavarian volunteer forces under General von Epp, May 1 - 2.

May 7. Allies presented treaty which included League of Nations Covenant to Germans.

May 29. Comprehensive German counterproposals transmitted to Allies. Allied reply received on June 16.

July 31. Weimar Constitution passed by National Assembly with controversial Article 48 giving President power to restore order whenever state failed to abide by federal constitution.

December. Hitler, who was army propaganda officer, was sent to investigate German Workers' Party. He was so intrigued that he became member of Party with membership number 7.

December 4. Mass meeting of all parties in Cologne. Mayor of Cologne, Dr. Konrad Adenauer, stepped into national limelight as chairman of committee of all parties.

1920   February 24. First mass meeting of German Workers' Party at which Hitler announced new name: National Socialist German Workers' Party (NSDAP) and proclaimed 25 Point Program designed by Gottfried Feder.

March 12. Kapp Putsch occurred because of decision to
eliminate free corps from army. Wolfgang Kapp made
himself Chancellor and Prussian Prime Minister, but the
army in the south and west refused to cooperate with him.
Kapp fled four days later when he realized that he could
not succeed.

March 19. Armed revolution began in Ruhr largely
brought on by Communist leaders. Reichswehr troops
began reconquest of Ruhr on April 2.

April 1. Hitler left the army, making the organization
of the party his full-time business.

June 6. Reichstag elections held. Weimar coalition did not
even win a simple majority.

December. Nazi Party bought weekly paper Volkische
Beobachter.

1921   January 1. Reduction of army to 100,000 men as required
by Versailles Treaty offered opportunity to remove all
soldiers who had republican inclinations.

April 27. Allied governments established German obligation to make reparations payments of 42 annuities
ranging from 2 to 6 billion marks.

May. Russo-German trade treaty concluded.

August. Nazis definitively organized SA as "Gymnastic
and Sports Division" within the Party. Changed name to
Sturmabteilung.

August 26. Matthias Erzberger was fatally shot by two
former members of Ehrhardt brigade. Reich President
used Article 48 to temporarily forbid anti-republican
publications, meetings and organizations.

October 20. League of Nations Council announced its
decision to assign 40% of Upper Silesia which contained
Polish majority to Poland.

1922   April 16. Rapallo Treaty signed between Germans and
Russians. Two signatories waived all mutual claims
for compensation of wartime damages. They also
promised to boost their mutual trade.

October 11. <u>Reichstag</u> passed law extending term of President Ebert's service until July 1925 in order to avoid any further public unrest.

October 22 - 24. Serious uprising of Communists in Hamburg suppressed by police with great difficulty.

November 22. New Cabinet formed. Members did not have any clear identifiable party affiliation. Chancellor was William Cuno.

December 27. Reparation Commission with exception of British member declared Germany in default of her reparations payments.

1923   January 11. France invaded Ruhr claiming that Germans were not meeting their reparations obligations. Met by passive resistance with German government assuming cost of mounting subsidies and compensation for population.

August 12. William Cuno forced to resign.

August 13. "Great coalition" government formed by Gustav Stresemann.

September 26. Stresemann announced termination of German resistance in Ruhr. President Ebert used Article 48 to declare state of emergency. Angered nationalists.

October 3. Cabinet forced to resign because of great opposition.

October 6. Gustav Stresemann presented new cabinet to Reichstag with Communists and Nationaists in opposition.

October 13. <u>Reichstag</u> enacted law giving government plenary powers to deal with crisis over Ruhr occupation and currency inflation.

October 16. Government acted to end monetary crisis by establishing new bank of issue and decreed introduction of new currency.

November 12. Hjalmar Schacht made special currency commissar and helped stabilize German currency by halting printing of worthless paper money.

November 8. Munich Beer Hall Putsch carried out by Adolph Hitler and his followers. General Ludendorff joined them. State police stopped Nazis as they marched into the city. President Ebert gave full dictatorial power to General von Seeckt under Article 48. Hitler was eventually arrested, tried and sentenced to prison.

1924   Thomas Mann published Magic Mountain.

January 21. Conference of experts on reparations convened in Paris. Eventually produced Dawes Plan, named for Charles G. Dawes. Reduced amounts to be paid until 1928-29 when 2.5 billion mark payments to begin.

February. Stresemann offered German commitment to respect Western frontier as defined by Versailles Treaty.

February 26. Trial of Ludendorff and Hitler conducted. Ludendorff treated with deference. Hitler used trial to publicize his party's goals.

September 1. Dawes plan went into operation. New Reichsmark currency made its appearance and social conditions improved.

September 25. Note drafted by German government, indicating it wanted to be admitted to League with permanent seat on Council.

December. Hitler given amnesty.

Late December. Allied governments declared that would not evacuate Cologne zone on January 10, 1925, as originally planned under Versailles Treaty.

1925   February 28. President Ebert died.

April 11. Field Marshal Paul von Hindenburg was convinced to run for President.

April 26. Presidential election in which Field Marshal von Hindenburg had largest number of votes but not absolute majority. On second ballot only simple plurality was sufficient and Hindenburg was elected.

May 12. Hindenburg inducted as President.

July. Ruhr district cleared of foreign troops.

October 16. Statesmen of four big powers as well as Belgium, Czechoslovakia and Poland met in Locarno.

December 1. Locarno agreements officially signed in London and were to take effect as soon as Germany became member of League. Rhine Pact provided that existing boundaries should be inviolable. Germany made arbitration treaties with France, Belgium, Czechoslovakia and Poland.

1926   January 30. Allies completed evacuation of Cologne zone as promised on November 16.

April 24. Russo-German Treaty signed at Berlin by Stresemann and Chicherin, Russian Foreign Minister. Stated that Rapallo Treaty would remain basis of Russo-German relations, and in addition, the two countries would maintain friendly contacts in order to find an understanding on all political and economic questions. Reichstag ratified on June 30.

September 8. Germany admitted to League of Nations. Took seat as member of Council on September 10.

1927   January 31. Military Control Commission withdrawn from Germany, and all further supervision of armaments entrusted to Council of League.

April 6. Aristide Briand announced France's readiness to sign pact with United States outlawing war. Led to opening of widespread negotiations for multilateral agreement.

1928   May 20. German national elections held in which Hitler's Nazis, as well as Nationalists, suffered a slump.

August 17. Gustav Stresemann accepted French invitation to come to Paris to sign anti-war Pact. Historic occasion of German foreign minister in French capital.

August 27. Representatives of fifteen nations met at French Foreign Office to sign Treaty renouncing war as instrument of national policy.

1929

Hitler selected Heinrich Himmler (1900-1945) as leader of SS (Schutzstaffeln) which at that time consisted of 290 men but grew to 52,000 by 1933.

February 9. Committee of financial experts convened in Paris with Owen Young as Chairman. Submitted new plan (Young Plan) for reparations to German delegates on April 13.

May 4. Young suggested compromise plan which was finally accepted on June 7 by Hjalmar Schacht, Finance Minister. Germany established 59-year schedule of payments averaging 2.05 billion marks.

July 9. Alfred Hugenberg, Chairman of German Nationalist Party; Franz Seldte, leader of Stahlhelm; Heinrich Class, Chairman of Pan-German League and Adolph Hitler formed national committee that launched drive for plebiscite against Young Plan which was finally held in December with very little support.

August 6. Opening of Hague Conference on Reparations. Reached agreement on August 28 on reparations and that withdrawal of occupation forces would begin on September 15, 1929, to be completed not later than June 30, 1930.

September 15. Allied evacuation of Rhineland began.

October 3. Gustav Stresemann died.

1930

January 16. Prussian Minister of the Interior, Albert Grzesinski, issued circular forbidding outdoor meetings and parades in order to stop demonstrations over deterioration of country's economic situation, especially Nazis.

March 13. Hindenburg signed measures to implement Young Plan.

March 18. Reichstag passed bill for protection of republic and for suppression of political disturbances.

June 30. Berlin government issued proclamation to
people of the Rhineland after removal of Allied troops
ahead of schedule, stressing burdens Germany had faced
to free the territory.

July 16. Bruning government, which had come into power
on April 1, was defeated in its economic program. Bruning then issued the entire program as presidential emergency decree under Article 48 of the Constitution.

July 18. Reichstag dissolved.

September 14. Elections held. Division in German
Nationalist camp worked in favor of Nazis. Foreign
creditors became alarmed and withdrew 420 billion marks
by September 26.

1931   May 11. Creditanstalt, greatest Austrian banking house,
became insolvent.

June 5 - 8. British Government invited Bruning and Cur-
tius to meet with Prime Minister Ramsay MacDonald and
Foreign Secretary Arthur Henderson. They convinced
Germans to delay actions on moratorium of Young Plan
payments until arrival in Europe of United States Secretary of State Henry L. Stimson.

June 20. German government proposed moratorium on
payments of all intergovernmental debts.

July 6. Agreements reached in Paris whereby annual in-
stallment of reparations debt had to be paid by Germany
in 1931-32 but would immediately be given as loan to German railroad company by Bank of International Settlement.

Summer. General von Schleicher opened negotiations
with Nazi Party to see what conditions would be necessary
for it to join the government in order to avoid civil war
in Germany.

September 3. German Foreign Minister had announced
abandonment of proposed Austro-German Customs Union
because of opposition of France, Italy and Czechoslovakia.

September 18. Hitler's niece, Geli, was found shot dead
in her room. State attorney said it was suicide.

1932

January 27. Hitler delivered speech before tycoons of
Rhenish and Ruhr industries which won support of many
for Nazi Party.

February 22. Goebbels proclaimed Hitler's candidacy
for Presidency.

March 18. Presidential elections held. Hindenburg won
46.6% of vote, and Hitler, 30.1%.

April 10. Runoff election for Presidency held. Hindenburg received 53% of vote, and Hitler, 36.8%.

April 13   New elections in 4/5 of German states confirmed results of second Hindenburg election meant end
of Parliamentary government on state level.

May 30. Bruning received news from Geneva that United
States, Great Britain, Italy and even France would grant
equality in armaments to Germany.

May 31. Franz von Papen accepted office of Chancellor
after President Hindenburg appealed to his patriotism.

June. Reparations Conference met at Lausanne. Germany to make one last payment and then debt to be cancelled. Papen openly declared his opposition to make
even one more payment.

June 16. Presidential decree lifted ban on para-military
organizations of Nazi Party.

July 31. Federal elections held in which Nazis doubled
vote and membership in parliament compared to 1930, but
failed to gain majority. New Reichstag, 52% of seats
held by two totalitarian parties: Nazis and Communists.

August 9. Government established special courts to deal
with excesses in demonstrations by introducing high
penalties against violators. When Nazi Storm Troopers
beat Communist worker to death in Upper Silesia on
August 10, a special court condemned the five murderers
to death. Nazis protested and Hitler justified the murder.

August 13. Hitler met with General Hindenburg and
Papen. Latter two prepared to offer Hitler Vice-Chan-
cellorship and Prussian Ministry of Interior for one of
his lieutenants. Hitler rejected offer and lost his
temper. Said he wanted coalition government but gave
impression was claiming dictatorship.

August 30. Parliament assembled; elected Hermann
Goring, Speaker, then adjourned until September 12.

November 6. New elections: Nazis won only 33.1% of
vote, down from 37.2%.

December 3. General von Schleicher assumed task of
forming new cabinet.

December 6. Parliament assembled -- last session of
Reichstag in Weimar Republic.

December 8. Gregor Strasser resigned from Nazi Party,
tried to organize own following within Party.

THE THIRD REICH: NAZI DICTATORSHIP

1933   January 4. Papen met Hitler in Cologne at home of
wealthy banker, Baron von Schroeder. Hitler agreed to
Papen's proposal to join with German Nationalists.

January 28. General von Schleicher resigned at noon.
President Hindenburg agreed to formation of rightist
cabinet, commissioning Papen to conduct negotiations
with Hitler and Hugenberg.

January 30. Hitler and members of cabinet took office.

February 3. Hitler addressed commanders of German
army, telling them that true aim of German policy was
to regain political power.

February 4. First emergency decree giving Hitler dis-
cretion to limit right of assembly and of the press.

February 27. Reichstag building caught on fire. Nazis
claimed that Communists caused fire as signal of general
revolt of Communisim in Germany. Served as screen for
emergency decree of February 28 to defend state against
Communist violence.

March. Austrian Chancellor, Engelbert Dollfuss (1892-
1934) suspended the parliamentary constitution.

March 5. Nazis received 43.9% of popular vote in elections. 8% vote of Nationalists gave Hitler bare majority
of 52%. Nazis claimed this was grand victory for Party.

March 12. Presidential directive abolished black, red
and gold flag and ordered display of black, white and red
flag of Bismarckian Empire with Swastika flag of Nazi
Party.

March 21. Opening of new Reichstag which passed Enabling
Act. Reichsrat passed it in evening. Hitler now independent of Hindenburg as well as of German Nationalists--
was now dictatorial ruler of Germany.

Spring. Germany renewed Treaty of Berlin of 1926 with
Russia.

April 1. Anti-Jewish pogroms and demonstrations conducted

April 7. Law passed to purge officialdom of Jewish and
non-Aryan elements.

April 10. Law enacted, declaring May 1 "the day of
national labor"

May 1. All workers marched to meeting places where
were addressed by Nazi leaders.

May 2. Nazi Storm Troopers took over all organs of
free trade unions.

May 10. Book burning organized at Berlin Opera Square
sounding keynote for cultural policies of Third Reich.

New German Labor Front (DAF) held first national
congress.

May 17. Hitler delivered most effective peace speech.

May 27. German government made passport visas to
Austria dependent on payment of 1,000 marks in order to
wreck Austrian tourist trade.

June. Austrian government banned Nazi Party completely.

Hitler appointed Baldur von Schirach "Youth Leader of the German Empire."

July 14. Law issued making National Socialist German Workers' Party the only political party in Germany.

July 20. Hitler concluded Concordat with Vatican.

Early Summer. Special concentration camps opened.

October 14. Hitler withdrew German Reich from League of Nations.

December 1. Issued "The Law for Safeguarding the Unity of Party and State." Nazi Party was tied to state. Leaders of Party to be members of Cabinet in order to guarantee cooperation of Party and State.

1934
January 26. Hitler signed 10-year pact with Poland. Two states promised to settle issues between them diplomatically and not to resort to force.

February 27. Benito Mussolini (1883-1945) of Italy joined France and England in joint declaration on necessity of preserving Austrian independence and integrity.

March 17. Mussolini signed Rome Protocols with Austria and Hungary. Projected closer economic relations as well as common general policies.

June 14 - 15. First meeting between Hitler and Mussolini took place in Venice.

June 30 - July 1. S.A. purged. Ernst Rohm arrested and executed after he refused to commit suicide. Moral defamation charge of homosexuality added.

July 25. Austrian Nazis succeeded in killing Chancellor Dollfuss. Leaders and several thousand of their followers had taken refuge in Germany.

August 2. Reich President von Hindenburg died at age
of 87. Even before his death, Reich government decided
to incorporate office of President with that of Chancellor.

1935   January 13. Saar Plebiscite gave visible sign of success
of Nazi regime's foreign policy when people overwhelm-
ingly voted to rejoin with Germany.

March 16. Hitler announced introduction of compulsory
military service, providing for peacetime army of
550,000 men.

April 11. Stresa Conference attended by Britain, France
and Italy, reaffirming their search for collective security
in Eastern Europe, air pact in the west, independence
of Austria and disarmament.

May 21. Hitler delivered "peace speech" criticizing
League of Nations and mania for collective security.
Denied any German plans of conquest, including annexa-
tion of Austria.

June 18. Anglo-German Naval Treaty signed allowing Ger-
man navy to be 35% of size of British navy, but permitting
Germany to have equal number of submarines as
British Commonwealth.

September 15. Nazi Party Convention announced passage
of Nuremberg laws defining Jews as anyone having 3
Jewish grandparents, although number later reduced to
2. All Jews were deprived of rights of citizens, were to
be considered only subjects of Reich. Forbade intermarriage with Jews, as well as extra-marital intercourse between two races.

1936   March 7. Units of German army mached into Rhineland
in morning - flagrant breach of Articles 42 and 44 of
Versailles Treaty. French could have stopped advance.

July 16. Outbreak of Civil War in Spain. Germans and
Italians contributed to Franco's cause, using it as
opportunity to try out weapons.

July 11. Chancellor Kurt von Schusnigg of Austria
felt compelled to sign agreement with Germany in
which latter recognized sovereignty of Austria, promising not to interfere in her internal affairs. Austria
would maintain her policies as German state. In
secret article, Austria gave assurance that Nazi opposition would receive representation in government.

August. Olympic Games held in Berlin.

November 25. Germany signed Anti-Comintern Treaty
with Japan. Published part of Treaty indicated that
partners would inform each other of Communist International and would consult and cooperate on defense
measures. Secret supplementary agreement committed
each to neutrality should the other go to war with
Soviet Union.

1937

March 14. Pope Pius IX issued encyclical "With Burning Sorrow" in which he charged Nazis with having
violated Concordat and condemned Teutonic folk here-
sies promoted by Rosenberg.

June 24. Field Marshal von Blomberg gave "Top
Secret" Directive to three Service Chiefs concerning
Germany's plans for conquest.

September 23. Mussolini left for Germany to meet
Hitler at Munich.

November 5. Hitler signed minorities treaty with
Poland.

    Hitler disclosed his thoughts to Field-Marshal Blom-
berg, German War Minister; Colonel-General von Fritsch,
Commander-in-Chief of Army; Admiral Raeder,
Commander-in-Chief of Navy; Göring, Commander-in-
Chief of Air Force and Neurath, German Foreign Minister. Indicated that aim of German policy was to
secure and preserve racial community, to enlarge it,
that is to gain living space (Lebensraum) to the East.

1938

January 25. Hitler took opportunity to get rid of General
Blomberg. Had married woman whom Himmler and
Göring showed once registered as prostitute. Generals
demanded Blomberg's resignation. Himmler and Göring

also produced put-up charge of homosexuality against
General von Fritsch. Then Hitler able to appoint
General Wilhelm Keitel (1882-1946) and new high
command (OKW) which in effect became Hitler's personal military staff.

Police raid on Austrian Nazi headquarters in Vienna
brought out plans for rising in Spring of 1938 and for
appeal to Hitler to intervene.

February 12. Hitler browbeat Austrian Chancellor
Schusnigg into delivering Austria into Hitler's hands.
Arthur Seyss-Inquart (1892-1946), Nazi collaborator, to
be made Minister of Interior.

March 9. Schusnigg announced plebiscite in four days
for independent Austria. Hitler then ordered army to
prepare to invade Austria on March 10. Hitler informed
Mussolini of his intention to intervene in Austria because of persecution of pro-German Austrians and
threat of military cooperation between Austria and
Czechoslovakia.

March 12. German troops marched into Austria.
Hitler went to Linz in evening and to Vienna on March
13.

March 14. Law promulgated making Austria province
of Reich.

March 28. Konrad Henlein, Sudeten Nazi leader, had
three hour conference with Hitler, Ribbentrop and
Rudolph Hess in Berlin. Henlein was told to consider
self representative of Fuhrer and to put forward demands which would be unacceptable to Czech government.

April. Nazi government ordered registration of Jewish
commercial business.

April 12. General Keitel received orders to draft
plans for invasion of Czechoslovakia.

May 20. Czechs ordered partial mobilization of army.
British and French diplomats warned Hitler that German aggression might lead to general war.

May 28. Hitler announced to leaders of Party and armed forces his intention to smash Czechoslovakia to pieces.

May 30. German army ordered to prepare for military attack against Czechoslovakia after October 1.

June 22. Special decree instituted labor conscription.

September 13. Henlein, Nazi leader of Sudeten Germans broke off negotiations with Czech government leading to revolt in many parts of Sudetenland.

September 15. Neville Chamberlain, British Prime Minister, made first plane trip to Berchtesgaden. Offered to cede Sudeten territories to Germany, then had to convince his cabinet, the French and Czechs.

September 22. Chamberlain flew to Godesberg, Germany to meet Hitler. When Chamberlain informed him of agreement on cession of Sudetenland, Hitler demanded more: immediate withdrawal of Czechs from Sudetenland. Also gave assurance that this was last territorial demand he would make in Europe.

September 29 - 30. Munich Conference attended by German and Italian dictators and British and French Prime Ministers. Germans gained Sudetenland with promise of plebiscite to determine what parts to remain German - never took place.

October 5. Jews had to register all their financial possessions which amounted to more than 5,000 marks.

October 21. Armed forces ordered to prepare for disposal of rump Czechoslovakia.

October 24. Ribbentrop began negotiations with Polish Ambassador, offering Poland "total solution" of all pending problems.

November 7. Herschel Grynspan, son of one of Polish Jews made stateless, shot Ernst von Rath, one of secretaries of German Embassy in Paris. Served as excuse for Goebbels to move anti-Semitic propaganda into high gear.

November 9 - 10. Reichskristallnacht (Night of Crystal):
SA men out of uniform, attacked and destroyed Jewish
homes, temples and businesses. 20,000 Jews arrested
and thrown into concentration camps. On November 12,
Jews were ordered to repair damage on their own because
insurance claims were seized by government. Had to
pay 1 billion marks, and other punitive measures issued
against Jews.

December 6. German and French foreign ministers
signed treaty promising good neighborly relations.

1939   March 14 - 15. Czech President Hacha and foreign minister forced to turn over government of country to Hitler.

March 10. Hitler proclaimed in Prague establishment of
German Protectorate.

May 22. "Pact of Steel" signed in Berlin Chancellory en-
visaging close political and economic cooperation.

May 23. Hitler met with senior armed forces officers in
Reich Chancellery, telling them to prepare for attack on
Poland.

August 23. Nazi-Soviet nonaggression pact signed.

September 1.   Germans invaded Poland, leading to outbreak of World War II. Warsaw surrendered on September 27.

September 28. German-Soviet Boundary and Friendship
Treaty confirmed division of Poland, providing for re-
settlement of Baltic Germans.

October 7. Hitler appointed Himmler head of new organization, R.K.F.D.V., Reich Commissariat for strengthening of German Folkdom. First task to deport Poles
and Jews from provinces annexed to Germany.

1940   January 10. Hitler ordered attack on West for 17th. But
German Air Force Staff Officer made forced landing in
Belgium while flying from Munich to Cologne. Had with
him complete operational plan for offensive. Delayed
plans until after winter.

March 2. United States Under-Secretary of State, Sumner Welles, visited Berlin to sound out possibilities for peace before conflict began in earnest.

April 9. Germans made surprise attack on Norway and Denmark eventually occupying both. British fleet was on way to mine Norwegian waters.

May 10. German army invaded Low Countries and France.

June 17. Hitler received French plea for armistice and danced with joy.

June 21. French signed armistice with Germans in same railroad car and at exact place in Forest of Compiegne, northeast of Paris where General Foch had dictated terms of capitulation to German delegation on November 11, 1918.

August 13. German aircraft opened "Operation Eagle" designed to eliminate R.A.F.

September 7. German Air Force began attacks on London as retaliation for attack on Berlin.

September 17. "Operation Sea-Lion" (attack on Britain) postponed and was finally cancelled January 1942.

October 4. Hitler and Mussolini met on Brenner Pass to discuss problems involved with Spanish intervention.

October 23. Hitler and Generalissimo Franco met at Spanish frontier. Franco hesitant about Spanish participation in war in order for Germans to take Gibraltar.

October 24. Hitler had successful interview with Marshal Petain at Montoire. Petain indicated readiness to accept principle of collaboration.

October 28. Italians attacked Greece in contradiction of Hitler's wishes.

December 18. Hitler issued directive indicating his intention to attack Russia.

1941   January 19 - 20. Mussolini visited Berghof. Received
            fairly good reception. Hitler indicated his coming inter-
            vention in Greece. Concealed plans for "Barbarossa"
            attack against Russia.

            April 6. Germans launched attack against Yugoslavia.
            Capitulated on April 17.

            April 23. Greeks finally surrendered after six months'
            heroic resistance.

            May 10. 5:45 P.M. Rudolph Hess flew Messerschmidt
            fighter toward Scotland to meet with Duke of Hamilton,
            whom he had met at Olympic Games of 1936, to negotiate
            peace between Germany and Britain. Hess was arrested
            and remained in prison throughout the war. Hitler was
            shocked and angered at what he had done.

            June 18. Non-Agression Pact signed between Germany and
            Turkey.

            June 22. Dawn. Hitler's forces attacked Russia.

            December 6. Russians launched major counter-offensive
            along whole Central Front with 100 fresh divisions sweep-
            ing away German threat to Moscow.

            December 7. Japanese bombed Pearl Harbor in surprise
            attack.

            December 11. In abusive speech, Hitler announced Ger-
            many's declaration of war on America.

1942   February. Hitler appointed young architect, Albert
            Speer, Minister for Armaments and Munitions, in place
            of Dr. Todt, who was killed in air accident.

            Spring. Efficient main office in Berlin began to supply
            gas vans for mobile extermination to concentration camps.

            June 30. Afrika Korps reached El Alamein line, 65 miles
            from Alexandria, Egypt.

            November 7 - 8. British and American troops landed
            along coast of Morocco and Algeria, within few days oc-
            cupied whole of French North Africa to Tunisian frontier.

1943   May 7. Allies captured Tunis and Bizerta in Africa and
            then entire Axis forces.

            July 12. Russians able to take offensive against Germans.

            July 19. Hitler summoned Mussolini to meeting in nor-
            thern Italy to renew strength of alliance, but made no
            promise of reinforcements to Italians.

            July 25. Mussolini dismissed by King after meeting of
            Fascist Grand Council. Mussolini placed under arrest.
            Marshal Badoglio formed non-Fascist government.

            September 8. Badoglio Government arranged armistice
            with Allies.

            September 10. Report of striking successes for Germans
            in Italy against Allies.

            September. Spectacular air rescue of Mussolini by SS
            detachment under Otto Skorzeny, brought Duce to Fuhrer's
            Headquarters at Rastenberg. Proclaimed Mussolini's
            restoration to leadership of Fascism on September 15.

1944   June 4. Allies captured Rome.

            June 6. Allies invaded Normandy catching Germans un-
            awares.

            July 20. Colonel Claus Schenk von Stauffenberg flew to
            Hitler's East Prussia headquarters for conference.
            Placed briefcase with bomb under table and left on excuse
            of telephone call to Berlin. 12:42 P.M. blast shattered
            room. Hitler was injured, but had been protected by
            table top and heavy wooden support against which Stauffen-
            berg's briefcase had been pushed. Hitler claimed that
            his safety was sign from heaven.

            July 21. 12:30 A.M. Fuhrer addressed Germans, assur-
            ing them of his safety and explaining what occurred.
            Assassination attempt changed Hitler's relationship with
            army which was no longer allowed position of independ-
            ence.

            August 24. Goebbels announced total mobilization.

September 11. Evening. American patrol crossed German frontier.

December 10. Hitler left Berlin where he had been since
November and went to "Eagle's Nest", his field headquarters in West.

1945   March 7. Americans and British crossed Rhine River.

April 12. President Franklin D. Roosevelt died. German
hopes were raised that this would lead to a weakening of
Allied resolve.

April 21. Hitler ordered all-out attack on Russians be-
sieging Berlin -- never launched.

April 22. Hitler decided to remain in Berlin, indicated
that war was lost.

April 26. Russians began to shell Chancellery.

        Göring relieved of command of Luftwaffe, replaced
by Colonel-General Robert Ritter.

April 28. Hitler was informed that Himmler had been
in touch with Swedish Count Bernadotte for purpose of
negotiating peace terms. Ordered Himmler's arrest
on April 29.

April 28. Allied military mission described Buchenwald
concentration camp as "extermination factory".

April 29. Hitler married Eva Braun, then wrote his
political testament justifying his position and decisions.
Named Admiral Doenitz his successor.

April 30. Eva and Adolph Hitler committed suicide.
Their bodies were cremated in Chancellery Garden.

May 2. Russians captured Berlin.

May 4. Admiral von Friedeburg signed armistice providing for surrender of German forces in northwest
Europe.

May 5. Admiral Doenitz indicated senseless struggle against Western allies but urged continuation of war against Russia.

May 7. General Jodl and Admiral Friedeburg signed unconditional surrender of all German forces.

POSTWAR GERMANY

May 9. Reichmarshal Hermann Göring gave self up to United States 7th Army.

May 23. Admiral Doenitz' government dissolved by Allied authorities, all members of government under arrest.

Heinrich Himmler commited suicide by poison.

June 5. German Reich under full control of United Nations.

June 9. Allied military authorities disclosed that Nazis had exterminated at least 80% of Germany's Jews.

August 29. Hermann Göring, Joachim von Ribbentrop, Hjalmar Schacht and 21 other Nazi civilian and military leaders indicted by Allied jurists as war criminals.

September 17. Josef Kramer and 44 SS aides on trial in British military court on charges of conspiracy to commit mass murder in Nazi concentration camps at Bensen and Oswiecim.

September. Allied Proclamation declared Nazi Party illegal and ordered abolition of all German armed forces and semi-military organizations.

September 29. President Truman released survey made by Earl G. Harrison that United States occupation authorities were treating Jews as Nazis had. Directed General Eisenhower to alleviate the "shocking" treatment of displaced Jews in Germany.

October 1. All restrictions on fraternizing between Allied soldiers and Germans except for certain bans on intermarriage relaxed by Allied control council.

October 12. General Eisenhower made announcement
that Nazi Party members would be deprived of vote.

November 30. Rudolf Hess threw verbal bombshell at
Nuremberg War Criminals Trial when confessed that
he had been shamming insanity and amnesia for "tactical"
reasons.

December 1. Many German industrialists who aided
Hitler's rise to power arrested by British authorities in
Ruhr area.

December 14. Josef Kramer, Irma Grese and 9 others,
convicted for crimes committed at Belsen and Oswiecim
Concentration camps, were hanged.

1946   March 13. Hermann Göring admitted at Nuremberg trial
that he did everything in his power to strengthen Nazi
movement and assure Hitler his place as Chancellor.

March 20. Starving Germans in Hamburg started food
riots, looting food shops and railroad cars.

March 30. About 800 Germans arrested in United States
and British zones in Austria and Germany in raid designed to crush attempt of some Nazis to revive party.

April 30. Hjalmar Schacht told International Military Tribunal that Hitler had deceived the world, Germany and
him, implied that history would remember Schacht as
ardent German pacifist.

May 13. Allied military government of Germany ordered
destruction by January 1 of all German military and Nazi
memorials and confiscation of all books glorifying naziism
or militarism.

Fifty-eight operators of Mauthausen concentration
camp convicted by U.S. military court in Dachau for tor-
ture and murder of thousands of imprisoned victims, and
sentenced to death.

August 31. 20 of 22 Nazi defendents on trial at Nuremberg
for war crimes protested their innocence in final pleas.
Hans Frank publicly confessed blame for atrocities laid
to him; Martin Bormann was being tried in absentia.

October 1. Nazi defendents convicted of war crimes sentenced to death by International Military Tribunal; 3 received life sentences; 4 given lighter sentences and 3 acquitted: Franz von Papen, Hjalmar Schacht and Hans Fritsche.

October 16. 10 leading Nazis convicted of crimes against humanity hanged in Nuremberg prison gymnasium. Hermann Göring committed suicide by swallowing poison two hours before being hung.

December 2. Anglo-U. S. Pact for economic merger of respective zones in Germany signed by Secretary of State Byrnes and Foreign Minister Bevin.

1947

February 23. Allied intelligence agents arrested several hundred leaders of Nazi underground movements in British and United States zones of Germany.

February 24. Franz von Papen sentenced to 8 years in labor camp after German denazification court found him guilty of being major Nazi offender.

February 27. Herbert Hoover urged United States and Britain each to allot $475.5 million to save Germany from starvation and chaos.

March 11. Secretary of State Marshall answered Soviet Foreign Minister Molotov's criticism of Anglo-American conduct of demilitarization by warning that only Allied unity could keep Germany disarmed.

March 17. Russian Foreign Minister Molotov asked for annulment of economic merger of American and British zones at Moscow meeting of Foreign Ministers.

March 19. Secretary of State Marshall warned France and Russia at Big Four Conference that rebuilding of German industry to pay for reparations would endanger peace.

March 22. Secretary of State Marshall proposed early establishment of German National Council to rule as provisional government at Moscow Conference.

March 29. German food demonstrations in British zone
spread to Ruhr.

April 12. Big Four Ministers in Moscow agreed that
German land reform would be completed by end of 1947,
and that major German war plants be destroyed by June
30, 1948.

April 18. British naval authorities destroyed German
naval base at Heligoland.

April 24. Moscow Council of Foreign Ministers concluded meetings with agreement to cut size of occupation
forces in Germany by September 1.

May 10. 12 German generals indicted on charges of having committed war crimes in Norway, Yugoslavia and
Albania.

May 14. United States War Department announced emergency plans to rush more than 1.2 million tons of food to
United States and British zones of Germany.

June 5. In Harvard University commencement address,
Secretary of State Marshall proposed that United States
help Europe solve its economic ills, provided that European countries adopt joint program. The Marshall Plan
later became known as the European Recovery Program.

July 3. Ernest Bevin and Georges Bidault, British and
French foreign ministers respectively, invited 22 Euro-
pean states to Paris conference on July 12 to discuss
French proposal on Marshall Plan aid to Europe.

July 12. Representatives of 16 nations opened conference
in Paris to work out program for European economic reconstruction under Marshall Plan, leaving door open for
participation of other nations.

July 15. Joint Chiefs of Staff issued new directives to
General Lucius D. Clay, Commander of United States
Zone of Germany, to take steps to stabilize political and
economic conditions in order to enable Germany to make
maximum contributions to European recovery.

August 22. Opening of Anglo-French-American Conference in London to discuss steps to increase industrial
production in Anglo-American zones of Germany.

August 29. Plan announced in Berlin to increase indus-
trial production in merged zones of United States and
Britain. Denounced on August 30 by Soviet Military
Governor Marshal Vassily D.Sokolovski.

September 19. European conferees on Marshall Plan
adopted report indicating that Western European trading
area would need over $19.3 billion from American coun-
tries during next four years.

September 22. Conclusion of 16-nation European conference on Marshall Plan with signing and dispatching of
requests for economic aid to Washington.

December 11. London Council of Foreign Ministers meeting since November 25, agreed to set level of German
steel output at 11.5 million ingot tons annually.

December 17. United States agreed to pay most of cost
of running Anglo-American zone of Germany in return
for controlling voice in zone's economic affairs.

December 19. President Truman asked Congress to
authorize $17 billion over 4-year period to support
European Recovery Program.

1948   January 8. British and United States military governors
announced acceptance by West German political leaders
of 6 proposals, giving Germans greater responsibility in
administration of the two zones.

February 6. All-German bi-zonal economic administration authorized by Anglo-United States proclamation giving enlarged powers to new regime.

February 13. Marshal Vasily D. Sokolovski announced
establishment of new economic advisory commission in
Russian zone comparable to U.S.-U.K. bizonal structure,
except that Soviet authorities appointed all members.

February 14. United States and British military governors decided to permit Germans to resume manufacture
of virgin aluminum, prohibited under Potsdam agreement.

March 2. Hermann Puender, German Christian Democratic Leader, elected head of executive committee
(cabinet) of new German bizonal regime.

March 6. Communiqué of 6-nation London Conference
on Germany (U. S., U. K., France, Belgium, Netherlands and Luxemburg) indicated agreement in principle
on internationalization of Ruhr industrial area, association of Benelux nations in broad policy matters relating
to Germany, federal system of government for Germany
and closer economic ties of French and Anglo-American
zones.

March 16. European Economic Conference of 16 nations
ended 2-day plenary meeting at Paris by inviting 3 western zones of Germany to join work of conference and be
represented in its permanent organization.

March 20. Marshal Sokolovski led his delegation out of
Allied Control Council meeting in Berlin after 3 other
representatives refused to report on London Conference
on Germany.

March 25. Secretary of State Marshall indicated United
States would continue as joint occupant of Berlin.

March 31. United States and British military officials in
Berlin rejected Soviet proposals to put rail and road
traffic into Berlin under almost complete Russian control.

April 14. United States, British and French Zonal commanders adopted common policy for participation of
West Germany in European Recovery Program.

April 24. General Clay maintained that United States
would continue to follow terms of 1945 4-power accord
governing flights into Berlin after Russians announced intention to impose new restrictions on air traffic into
Berlin.

May 31. United States-British-French-Benelux Conference
on Germany in London announced agreement on plans for
setting up West German State early in 1949, for reestab-
lishing international authority to control Ruhr, and for
prevention of future German aggression by stationing
United States, British and French troops in Germany for
indefinite period.

June 18. Soviet occupation authorities issued order banning all motor, railway and pedestrian traffic between Berlin and western zones of Germany.

June 21. United States and British authorities in Berlin initiated airlift in order to maintain flow of passenger traffic and essential supplies to and from Berlin.

June 23. Soviet land and water blockade of Berlin completed by stopping rail freight traffic from Berlin to Helmstedt for "technical difficulties."

July 1. Soviet representatives withdrew from Allied Kommandatura for Berlin -- last 4-power governing in Germany.

Western military governors authorized West German provisional leaders to begin work toward formation of constitutional regime.

July 6. Western Allies sent similar notes to Russia indicating their determination to remain in Berlin and called on Russia to lift land and water blockade of western sectors of Berlin.

July 14. Soviet Union rejected Western protest on Berlin blockade maintaining that Powers had forfeited all legal status in Berlin by violating Yalta and Potsdam agreements.

July 26. United States and British officials ordered cessation of all rail traffic from Western zones of Germany to Russian zones.

August 2. Envoys of United States, Britain and France met in Moscow with Russian Premier Stalin and Foreign Minister Molotov to discuss Berlin situation.

August 26 - 27. Communist raids prevented Berlin's City Assembly from meeting.

August 31. Allied Military Governors of Germany met in Berlin, following 4-power directive to try to agree upon a common currency for Berlin.

September 1. Parliamentary Assembly charged with
writing provisional constitution for West Germany met
at Bonn.

September 6. German Communists, backed by Russian
troops, forced Berlin's City Assembly to surrender its
quarters in Soviet sector and move to British sector.

September 9. Russian troops fired on crowd of over
250,000 Germans in Berlin, who were protesting Soviet
and Communist activities. Communist sponsored
counter-demonstration in Berlin attracting crowd of only
80,000 - 100,000.

September 25. Soviet reply to final 3-Power note on
Berlin demanded control of all traffic between Berlin and
West Germany and virtual economic control of Berlin.

September 26. Western Powers issued joint communiquè
indicating decision to submit Berlin dispute to U.N.
Security Council. Did so September 29.

October 18. Agreement signed in Berlin, merging
French zone of Germany with Anglo-American bizone.

October 22. 6 neutral members of U.N. Security Council presented compromise resolution on Berlin, calling
for immediate lifting of blockade, exclusive use of
Soviet-zone currency in Berlin and convening of Council
of Foreign Ministers to renew negotiations on Germany.

October 24. Soviet-type "Constitution for all Germany"
adopted by Soviet Zone People's Council after 3-day meeting in Berlin.

October 27. Soviet authorities in Berlin threatened to
force down all United States and British planes flying
outside air corridors leading to Berlin from West Germany.

November 30. Division of Berlin into western and
Soviet sectors virtually completed by formation of rump
Communist-controlled city council in Soviet sector.

December 5. More than 80% of voters in western
sectors of Berlin turned out to vote in Communist-boy-
cotted city assembly elections.

December 7. Ernest Reuter, Socialist leader and anti-
Communist, elected Lord Mayor by West Berlin's City
assembly.

1949   January 10. U. S. Military Governor Clay reported in-
dications of revival of extreme German nationalism.

January 17. Three Western Powers indicated inauguration of tripartite Military Security Board to prevent revival of German militarism.

February 4. British and American authorities in Germany announced beginning of counterblockade barring
passage of trucks between Anglo-U.S. bizone and
Soviet zone.

March 20. Western deutschemark made only legal
tender in western sectors of Berlin.

March 29. General Vasili I. Chuilkov replaced Marshal
Sokolovski as Soviet Commander in Germany.

April 4. North Atlantic Treaty signed in Washington,
D. C., by representatives of U. S., Canada, Belgium,
Denmark, France, Great Britain, Iceland, Italy, Lux-
embourg, the Netherlands, Norway and Portugal.

April 10. German Parliamentary Council at Bonn was
handed text of statute defining authority to be retained
by 3 western states after inauguration of West German
Republic.

April 25. West German political leaders and western
Allies reached agreement on terms of constitution for
proposed German Federal Republic.

May 3. President Truman approved retirement of General Lucius D. Clay as United States Military Governor.

May 4. Representatives of United States, Britain,
France and Soviet Union met in New York and agreed to

end blockade and counter-blockade of Berlin as well as reconvening of Council of Foreign Ministers to discuss entire German question.

May 5. Statute creating Council of Europe signed in London by representatives of 10 western states.

May 8. Draft of new West German Constitution adopted by parliamentary council at Bonn. Bonn selected as capital, May 10.

May 12. Berlin blockade lifted 12:01 Berlin time.

May 18. John J. McCloy, President of International Bank for Reconstruction and Development, named first United States Civilian High Commissioner.

May 19. André Francois-Ponçet named France's first high Commissioner.

May 21. Constitution of Federal Republic of Germany into effect at midnight German time.

May 30. Russian Foreign Minister, Andrei Y. Vishinsky rejected Western proposals for unification of Germany by extending West German Constitution to entire state.

June 1. General Sir Brian H. Robertson, British Military Governor in Germany, was named Britain's first High Commissioner.

June 15. German authorities in West Berlin given control over most of city government activities except foreign or security questions.

June 20. Council of Foreign Ministers adjourned in Paris without reaching agreement on Germany.

July 9. Soviet authorities closed all zonal crossings except one to truck traffic bound for Berlin from Western Germany - reopened on July 25.

August 3. Council of Europe came into existence.

August 24. President Truman proclaimed North Atlantic Treaty into effect.

September. Theodore Heuss, leader of Free Democratic Party, elected first President of Federal Republic of Germany by Federal Assembly.

September 15. Konrad Adenauer, head of Christian Democratic Union, elected first Chancellor.

September 21. Allied High Commission formally superseded Military government in West Germany.

September 30. Allied airlift to Berlin officially terminated with 277,264th flight.

October 7. German Democratic Republic proclaimed in Soviet zone.

October 8. West and East German trade officials signed agreement for exchange of goods for 9-month period ending June 30, 1950.

October 10. USSR transferred all administrative functions of Soviet military authorities to German Democratic Republic.

October 11. Wilhelm Pieck elected President of German Democratic Republic.

October 12. Otto Grotewohl elected minister-president (premier) of German Democratic Republic with all cabinet posts going to veteran Communists.

November 4. West Germany and Saar recommended for admission as associate members to Council of Europe.

November 22. Chancellor Adenauer and Allied High Commissioners initialed agreement lifting many industrial and diplomatic restrictions on Federal Republic of Germany.

December 15. Agreement making West Germany full participant in European Recovery Program signed in Berlin.

1950

February 6. German Federal Republic stopped issuance
of licenses for export of iron and steel to East Germany.
Lifted embargo February 25.

March 3. Agreement signed in Paris giving France 50-
year lease on coal mines in the Saar.

March 22. German Federal Republic issued proposal
for unification of Germany based on nation-wide free
elections, freedom of press and elimination of interzonal
barriers.

May 8. Allied High Commission promulgated laws designed to prevent German rearmament.

May 12. Allied High Commission granted German Federal Republic greater freedom in fields of shipping and
shipbuilding.

May 21. Chancellor Adenauer pledged support of Germany for Schuman Plan for integration of German and
French heavy industry.

May 28. Rally of Free German Youth in East Berlin
reached climax without attempting threatened invasion
of West Berlin.

June 8. Allied High Commission authorized German
Federal Republic to negotiate and conclude international
treaties except those involving trade and payments, subject to veto of occupying powers.

June 15. Bundestag approved West Germany's membership
in Council of Europe.

June 20. Delegates of Belgium, France, West Germany,
Italy, Luxembourg and Netherlands met in Paris to consider French plan to pool Western Europe's heavy industry.

November 10. U.N. Food and Agriculture Organization
elected German Federal Republic to full membership.

December 4. West German Interior Ministry announced
plans for formation of special frontier protection corps
to prevent infiltration of undesirable elements.

December 18. Foreign and defense ministers of NATO Powers voted to establish integrated armed force for defense of Western Europe, including participation of West Germany.

1951

March 6. Allied High Commission announced granting of right to establish foreign ministry to West Germany.

April 2. Allied High Commission lifted most restrictions on military production in German Federal Republic.

April 18. Chancellor Adenauer signed treaty in Paris giving effect to Schuman plan to pool Western Europe's coal and steel production.

May 2. German Federal Republic made full member of the Council of Europe.

September 13. United States, British and French foreign ministers agreed upon use of West German troops in European army.

October 24. President Truman issued proclamation formally ending state of war with Germany pursuant to Congressional resolution.

November 22. United States, British, French and West German foreign ministers agreed on full domestic sovereignty for West Germany if it joined proposed European army.

1952

January 11. West German Bundestag ratified Schuman Plan Treaty. Bundesrat ratified same on February 1.

February 11 - 19. London Conference of United States, Great Britain, France and West Germany reached agreement on German rearmament.

February 26. West Germany agreed to contribute 11.25 billion Reichsmarks ($2.67 billion) per year toward Western defense.

March 5. East Germany shut off all electricity to West Berlin and Hamburg.

March 15. Judge Joachim Heppe of Lower Saxony Court ruled for first time in any West German court that Hitler's rule had been illegal, and that those who had tried to assassinate Hitler in 1944 were heroes and not traitors.

March 21. Conference on Jewish damage claims against Germany opened in the Hague.

April 30. General Dwight D. Eisenhower made farewell review of troops at Frankfort-on-the-Main.

May 1. East German President, Wilhelm Pieck, indicated that East Germany would have to rearm if West Germany did so.

May 27. West Germany, France, Belgium, Netherlands, U.K. and Luxembourg signed agreement to create European defense Community with joint European army.

East Germany announced that it would permit no special travel between West Germany and West Berlin except by special permit after May 30.

June 1. West Berlin residents barred from Soviet zone of Germany.

June 28 - 29. U. S. Secretary of State, Dean Acheson, visited West Berlin to reassure people of continued United States' support.

July 18. Western allies increased jeep patrols in Western sectors of Berlin to prevent more kidnappings by raiders from East Germany.

July 28. Allied High Commission notified Chancellor Adenauer of removal of restrictions on German steel production.

August 2. President Truman signed West German peace contract and protocol providing for inclusion of Germany in EDC.

October 29. Train carrying 8 United States tanks to West Berlin was stopped at border of Soviet Zone by Soviet authorities.

November 30. French-supported autonomous government of Saar won substantial victory in elections for
new parliament. (Elections had been opposed by West
Germany).

December 29. East German government announced dis-
solution of its propaganda office headed by Gerhart
Eisler, Communist leader who had escaped from United
States.

1953   January 12. President-Elect Eisenhower revealed selec-
tion of President James B Conant of Harvard University
as U. S. High Commissioner in Germany.

February 10. West German government banned neo-
Nazi secret society pledged to overthrow democracy in
Germany.

     European Coal and Steel Community went into opera-
tion.

May 28. Soviet control commission in Germany abolished. V. S. Semanov named Soviet High Commissioner.

July 12. Soviet Foreign Minister V. M. Molotov rejected
President Eisenhower's offer of food to East Germany.

July 21. East German Government announced that USSR
had extended credits equal to $57 million for purchase of
foods in second half of 1953.

August 20. United States and West Germany signed
agreement providing for return of number of former
German ships allocated to United States at end of World
War II.

August 23. Soviet government signed protocol with East
Germany cancelling reparations payments from January
1, 1954.

September 2. West German government announced
mobilization of 4 million young civilians and athletes to
combat Communist plot to sabotage forthcoming parliamentary elections.

November 25. East Germany discontinued its requirement of interzonal passes for travel between East and
West Germany.

1954   March 26. Soviet government announced that German
            Democratic Republic had become sovereign state but
            that Soviet troops would be stationed there temporarily.

            March 29. President Theodor Heuss of West Germany
            signed laws ratifying EDC and peace contract with
            Western Allies.

            July 17. Theodor Heuss reelected to second 5-year term
            as President of West Germany.

            July 22. Otto John, head of West German Bureau, charged
            with investigating subversive activity revealed to have
            disappeared into Soviet sector of Berlin. Granted politi-
            cal asylum on August 4.

            August 6. East German government accepted President
            Eisenhower's offer of free food for flood victims.

            August 30. EDC was in effect rejected by French National
            Assembly.

            October 2. 9-Power Conference in London signed agree-
            ment providing for political and military integration of
            West Germany in Europe on basis of Brussels Treaty
            of 1948.

            October 23. Agreements signed in Paris ending occupa-
            tion of West Germany, admitting it to NATO, and estab-
            lishing Western European Union.

            December 2. 8 East European Communist nations
            signed declaration warning that if West Germany entered
            Western European Defense Pact, they would also form
            combined force with joint head.

1955   January 25. Soviet Government formally ended state of
            War between USSR and Germany.

            February 27. West German Bundestag approved Paris
            agreements. Bundesrat approved ratification on March
            18.

            April 1. West German Lufthansa Air Line began regular
            passenger service on internal German routes.

April 28. James B. Conant, U. S. High Commissioner in Germany, nominated to be first U. S. Ambassador to German Federal Republic.

May 5. Federal Republic of Germany became sovereign state.

May 7. Council of Western European Union met in formal session for first time in Paris.

May 9. German Federal Republic formally admitted as 15th member of NATO at meeting of Council in Paris.

May 14. USSR, Albania, Bulgaria, Czechoslovakia, East Germany, Hungary, Poland and Rumania signed mutual defense treaty at Warsaw.

June 30. United States and West Germany signed agreement at Bonn on military aid to be furnished by United States for equipment of West German armed forces.

September 20. USSR and East Germany signed series of agreements in Moscow aimed at increasing power and authority of German Democratic Republic.

September 30. USSR and West Germany agreed to establish diplomatic relations.

October 6. West German Cabinet established civilian defense council to direct West German armed forces.

December 9. East German government announced that its own border police had replaced Soviet troops guarding its frontiers.

December 13. Otto John, who had defected to East, returned to German Federal Republic.

December 18. Saar Parliamentary elections won by pro-German parties.

December 25. Communist China and East Germany signed treaty of friendly cooperation in Peking.

1956

January 1. New West German army's first 6 company-size units established.

January 28. Warsaw Treaty nations accepted East German army into their defense organization.

February 13. West Germany and United States signed agreement for cooperation in research for peaceful uses of atomic energy.

March 30. East German armed forces made first public appearance in East Berlin.

June 5. France and Germany agreed on political integration of the Saar into West Germany by January 1, 1957.

July 1. East German government announced plan to reduce size of army from 120,000 to 90,000 men.

August 17. West German Constitutional Court outlawed Communist Party and its various front organizations.

1957

January 1. The Saar formally reunited with West Germany.

February 20. Government leaders of Belgium, France, West Germany, Italy, Luxembourg and Netherlands agreed on treaties for pooling of nuclear resources and for gradual introduction of common market without tariff barriers.

March 25. Agreements to create European Economic Community (EEC) and European Community of Atomic Energy (Euratom) signed.

July 1. First 3 of 12 projected West German divisions joined NATO.

December 20. 17 West European nations signed Paris agreement setting up nuclear energy agency to promote cooperation in peaceful uses of atomic energy.

1958

January. Treaties establishing EEC and Euratom into effect.

April 9. West Germany and USSR concluded in Moscow general repatriation and trade agreements.

May 7. West Germany granted ($95 million) credit for trade to United Arab Republic.

December 16. NATO Council pledged support to maintain American, British and French troops in West Berlin.

1959   January 1. Treaties went into effect for Common Market and Euratom.

May 11. Conference of foreign ministers of United States, France, Britain and USSR opened in Geneva with East and West Germany present as advisors. Deadlocked by May 18. Adjourned June 20.

July 1. Heinrich Luebke, Christian Democrat, was elected President of West Germany.

November 21. East Germany and USSR signed 6-year trade treaty.

1960   April 14. East German government announced completion of collectivization of agriculture in its territory.

May 3. West Germany and France signed treaties giving West Germany air, supply and weapon-testing bases in France.

August 16. East-West German trade agreement signed in Berlin. Cancelled September 30 because of East German trade restrictions.

September 12. Walter Ulbricht became Chairman of East German Council of State.

December 14. West European nations, United States and Canada signed agreements in Paris for creation of Organization for Economic Cooperation and Development.

December 29. East and West Germany reached agreement for continuation of trade between them during 1961.

1961   April 11. Beginning of trial of Adolph Eichmann by Israeli court in Jerusalem; principal charges dealing with crimes against Jewish people during World War II. Sentenced to death on December 15 after conviction by court. Executed May 31, 1962.

November 19. After many charges and counter-charges
by Eastern and Western Powers, as well as fleeing of
many refugees to West Berlin during 1961, East German
troops and workers began to fortify wall which separates
East and West Berlin.

December 25. President John F. Kennedy delivered
special broadcast reassuring West Berliners that
United States would continue to support them.

1962   August 17. East German guards slew Peter Fechter in
his attempt to cross Berlin Wall, led to incitement of
demonstrations by mob of 5,000 West Berliners who
also jeered at U. S. soldiers for not rescuing Fechter.

November 17. West German Cabinet crisis grew out of
controversy over October 27 arrest of publisher of news
magazine Der Spiegel who had criticized West Germany's
defenses. Was further heightened by Chancellor Adenauer's refusal to dismiss Defense Minister Franz Joseph
Strauss who was accused of violating the freedom of the
press by ordering the arrest.

December 7. West German Chancellor Adenauer
announced his intention to retire in fall of 1963.

1963   January 22. Signing of Franco-German Treaty providing for collaboration in foreign policy, defense and
cultural affairs.

February 7. Der Spiegel publisher, Rudolf Augstein,
released from prison.

April 23. West German Economics Minister, Ludwig
Erhard, nominated by Christian Democrats to succeed
Adenauer as Chancellor.

October 16. Ludwig Erhard elected to succeed Konrad
Adenauer as West German Chancellor

December 20. Residents of West Berlin allowed to
visit relatives in East Berlin under holiday pass agreement between East and West Germany.

1964   June 12. Soviet Union and East Germany signed 20-year treaty of friendship, mutual assistance and cooperation in Moscow.

July 1. President Heinrich Luebke of German Federal Republic elected to second 5-year term at meeting of Federal Assembly in Berlin.

September 23. West German Cabinet approved one-year agreement permitting West Berliners to visit East Berlin in certain holiday periods and at times of family crisis.

September 24. East German Parliament elected Willi Stoph to succeed deceased Otto Grotewohl as Premier.

November 14. United States and West Germany issued joint communiqué in Washington, indicating far-reaching military agreements.

1965   February 4. In major press conference, French President, Charles de Gaulle, called for reunification of Germany.

February 7. United Arab Republic Authorities warned West Germany that U.A.R. would break diplomatic relations if Germany continued to ship arms to Israel.

February 12. Chancellor Erhard confirmed that West Germany had halted military aid to Israel in deference to demands of U.A.R.

March 1. German Democratic Republic and U.A.R. signed agreements providing for equivalent of $100 million in East German aid.

March 7. West Germany announced it was trying to establish diplomatic relations with Israel. Israeli Cabinet approved establishment of diplomatic relations on March 14.

April 7. West German Bundestag held first session in West Berlin since 1958. Meeting preceded by several days of harassment of West Berlin by East Germany.

May 13. West Germany and Israel announced opening of full diplomatic relations. Arab states severed relations with West Germany as result.

November 25. East Germany agreed to allow West Berliners to visit East Germany during 2-week period at Christmastime.

1966   March 1. East Germany applied for U.N. membership.

October 1. Albert Speer, former Nazi Minister for Armaments and War Production, and Baldur von Schirach, leader of Hitler Youth, were released from Spandau War Crimes Prison in Berlin after 20 years' imprisonment.

October 27. West Germany's coalition government disintegrated with withdrawal of four Free Democrat ministers.

November 21. Alleged neo-Nazi National Democrat Pary of Bavarian State in West Germany made sizeable gains in state elections. Had also increased its representation in Hesse elections of November 6.

December 1. West German Bundestag elected Kurt Georg Kiesinger of Christian Democratic Party to succeed Ludwig Erhard as Chancellor; Willy Brandt of Social Democratic Party became vice-chancellor and foreign minister in coalition cabinet.

1967   April 19. Konrad Adenauer, first Chancellor of West Germany died at age of 91. Buried April 25. President Johnson attended funeral and conferred with Chancellor Kiesinger.

August 3. West Germany and Czechoslovakia made first formal agreement since World War II, signing treaty providing for exchange of trade missions with limited consular functions.

September 26. West Berlin Mayor, Heinrich Albertz, resigned because of increasing tensions stemming from harsh police action against student demonstrators.

October 1. National Democratic Party (NPD), extreme right wing party in West Germany made strong showing in Bremen elections.

October 19. Klaus Schutz, former State Secretary to Willy Brandt, elected Mayor of West Berlin.

1968

January 31. West Germany and Yugoslavia resumed diplomatic relations after break of ten years.

April 13. Chancellor Kurt Kiesinger warned in TV address of tougher police measures as demonstrations by left wing youths continued in many major cities. Disorders developed because of assassination attempt against student leader, Rudi Dutschke, on April 11.

April 14. West Berlin police broke up peace march of about 4,000 students.

April 28. Right-wing NPD received 10% of votes in election in Baden-Wurttemberg.

June 11. East Germany announced several regulations governing travel by West German citizens between West Germany and West Berlin. Denounced by 3 Western Powers on June 12.

1969

February 9. East Germany announced that West German Federal Assembly members going to West Berlin for Presidential elections would be prevented from crossing East German territory.

March 1. Border guards sealed main access routes to West Berlin for about two hours.

May 9. West German Cabinet decided against upward revaluation of mark as wave of currency speculation reached its peak.

May 30. West Germany altered its policy of automatically severing relations with government which granted diplomatic recognition to East Germany.

August 7 - 8. Meeting between Chancellor Kiesinger and President Richard M. Nixon in Washington concluded with announcement of establishment of communications "hot line" between two capitols.

October 3. West German Social Democrats and Free Democrats announced agreement on coalition government.

October 21. Willy Brandt elected Chancellor of West Germany.

October 24. West Germany revalued the mark.

November 25. West Germany formally proposed talks aimed at improving relations with Poland. Poland indicated willingness to begin talks on December 22.

1970   January 22. West German Chancellor, Willy Brandt, sent letter to East German Premier, Willi Stoph, proposing negotiations between two states.

February 5 - 6. Polish-West German talks began.

March 19. East and West German leaders conferred in Erfurt, East Germany at first meeting of heads of postwar German nations.

May 21. Chancellor Brandt and Premier Stoph held second meeting in Kassel, West Germany.

June 23. West Germany and Poland completed broad economic cooperation pact in Warsaw.

July 12. West-German treaty, renouncing force, signed in Moscow.

November 27. East and West Germany resumed talks on normalizing relations in East Berlin.

December 7. Polish-West German treaty, ending aggression, signed in Warsaw.

1971   January 31. Telephone service between East and West Berlin reestablished after 19 years.

May 2. Erich Honecker named first Secretary of East German Communist Party following Ulbricht's resignation because of old age and ill health.

September. Big Four Representatives signed agreement on status of Berlin to take effect when East and West Germany reached agreement on implementation. West Germany broke off talks with East Germany on September 9.

October 15. East German Council of Ministers sent memo to U.N. Secretary-General, U Thant, and member states, proposing membership for both Germanies.

October 20. Chancellor Brandt received Nobel Peace Prize for efforts to lessen East-West tensions.

December 4. Two Germanies announced agreement on transit arrangements through East Germany to Berlin; deadlocked on visiting rights.

1972   May 11 - 24. Wave of terrorist bombings swept through West Germany. Interior Minister, Dietrich Genscher, confirmed in TV interview on May 24 that suspects sought were linked to Baader-Meinhof gang of left anarchists.

June 1. State and federal police captured Andreas Baader and two leading members of urban guerrilla group. Called self Red Army Faction, claimed responsibility for series of bombings in May.

June 5. Chancellor Brandt announced donation of 150 million German marks (about $47 million) to establish U. S. foundation for European studies in gratitude for Marshall Plan aid.

August 26. XXth Olympiad opened in Munich by West German President, Gustav Heinemann.

September 5. 8 Arab terrorists, members of Black September organization captured 9 members of Israeli Olympic team, killing 2. 5 of terrorists and 9 Israelis were killed at end of 23 hour drama at military airport near Munich after were brought there in military helicopters. Munich police tried ambush in order to save Israelis. Israeli Premier expressed satisfaction of handling of affair by Germans on September 6.

September 6. Finland and East Germany signed preliminary agreement for establishment of diplomatic relations.

September 14. West Germany and Poland agreed to establish diplomatic relations.

September 22. Chancellor Brandt deliberately lost vote
of confidence in Bundestag in order to pave way for new
elections 10 months early. President Heinemann formally dissolved Parliament, setting November 19 as
date for new elections.

Shortly before confidence vote, Bundestag unanimously
ratified traffic treaty with East Germany and air trans-
portation pact with Soviet Union.

REFORM EDICT OF 1807

Napoleon's victories led to the humiliating Peace of Tilsit on July 9, 1807, which almost destroyed Prussia as a State. Under these circumstances Prince Karl vom und zu Stein, who was in the royal service proposed a thorough-going reform of the whole social structure. The basic aim of this reform is indicated in the extracts below.

(Source: Georg H. Pertz. Das Leben des Ministers Freiherrn vom Stein (Berlin, 1850), vol. II, pp. 23-27.)

We Frederick William by the grace of God King of Prussia hereby make known and proclaim

Since the establishment of peace we have been concerned with relieving the sunken condition of our loyal subjects, by the quickest possible reward and greatest possible improvement of the situation. We have considered that because of the widespread need, the means which are at our disposal would not be sufficient to help each individual, and even if they were sufficient to help each individual, we could not hope to accomplish our purpose. In addition, in accordance with the imperative demands of justice and with the principles of a wise economic policy, we should want to remove every obstacle, which, in the past, has prevented the individual from gaining that prosperity he was able to reach. We have further considered that the existing restrictions on ownership of landed property and on the personal states of the agriculture are at odds with our beneficent wishes and serve to handicap a powerful force that might be used in the restoration of agriculture. . . . It is our desire, therefore, to reduce both restrictions insofar as the common welfare demands, we therefore proclaim the following.

I. Freedom of Exchange of Property.

Every inhabitant of our States is to have the right, without any limitation upon the state, to own or mortgage landed property of any kind. . . . All privileges possessed up to this time by noble over citizen are completely abolished.

II. Free Choice of Occupation

Every noble is allowed, without any decline in his status, from this time on, to engage in citizen occupations, while every citizen is permitted to pass from citizen into peasant class and every peasant to pass into the citizen class.

* * *

Frederick William

Schrotter.   Stein.   Schrotter II.

THE CARLSBAD DECREES OF 1819

Count Metternich, chief Minister of Austria, was the conservative symbol of the age. His influence over German affairs was attested to by the issuance of the Carlsbad Decrees, which were a series of repressive legislation. They were passed as a result of the murder of Kotzebue by Karl Sand, a student, on March 23, 1819. The regulations provided for inspection and regulation of German university affairs, censorship, and even imprisonment of patriots who challenged the status quo. The various German states were required to maintain these regulations.

(The Annual Register, 1819 (London, 1820), pp. 155-169.)

Provisional Decree relative to the Measures to be taken concerning the Universities.

Sect. 1. The Sovereign shall make choice for each university of an extraordinary commissioner, furnished with suitable instructions and powers, residing in the place where the university is established; he may be either the actual curator, or any other person whom the government may think fit to appoint.

The duty of this commissioner shall be to watch over the most rigorous observation of the laws and disciplinary regulations; to observe carefully the spirit with which the professors and tutors are guided in their public and private lectures; to endeavour, without interfering directly in the scientific courses, or in the method of instruction, to give the instruction a salutary direction, suited to the future destiny of the students, and to devote a constant attention to every thing which may tend to the maintenance of morality, good order and decency among the youths.

Sect. 2. The governments of the states, members of the confederation, reciprocally engage to remove from their universities and other establishments of instruction, the professors and other public teachers, against whom it may be proved, that in departing from their duty, in overstepping the bounds of their duty, in abusing their legitimate influence over the minds of youth, by the propagation of pernicious dogmas, hostile to order and public tranquility, or in sapping the foundation of existing establishments, they have shown themselves incapable of executing the important functions entrusted to them, without any obstacle whatever being allowed to impede the measure taken against them, so long as the present decree shall remain in force, and until definitive arrangements on this point be adopted.

A professor or tutor thus excluded, cannot be admitted in any other state of the confederation to any other establishment of public instruction.

Sect. 3.   The laws long since, made against secret or unauthorized associations at the universities, shall be maintained in all their force and rigour, and shall be particularly extended with so much the more severity against the well-known society formed some years ago under the name of the General Burgenschaft, as it has for its basis an idea, absolutely inadmissible, of community and continued correspondence between the different universities.

The governments shall mutually engage to admit to no public employment any individuals who may continue or enter into any of those associations after the publication of the present decree.

Sect. 4.   No student who, by a decree of the Academic Senate confirmed by the government commissioner, or adopted on his application, shall be dismissed from a university, or who, in order to escape from such a sentence, shall withdraw himself, shall be received in any other university; and in general, no student shall be received at another university without a sufficient attestation of his good conduct at the university he has left.

Decree relative to the Measures for preventing the Abuses of the Press.

Sect. 1.   As long as the present decree shall be in force, no writing appearing in the form of a daily paper or periodical pamphlet, which does not contain more than 20 printed leaves, shall be issued from the press without the previous consent of the public authority.

The works not comprehended under this regulation shall continue to be regulated by the laws now existing, or which may be hereafter enacted; and if any work of the above-mentioned description shall give rise to a complaint on the part of any state of the confederation, the government to which the complaint may be addressed shall cause proceedings to be instituted in its name against the authors or editors of the said work.

Sect. 2.   Each government is at liberty to adopt, for the maintenance and execution of the present decree, those measures which may appear the most suitable; it being well understood that these measures must be recognized proper to fulfil the object of the principal regulation of Art. 1.

Sect. 3.   The present decree being called for by the necessity generally acknowledged of adopting some preventive measures against the abuse of the press in Germany, as long as this decree shall remain in force, the laws attributing to the tribunals the prosecution and punishment of the abuses and offences committed by the press, inasmuch as they apply to the writings specified in Art. 1, cannot be considered as sufficient in any state of the confederation.

Sect. 5.   In order that this responsibility, founded in the nature of the Germanic Union and inseparable from its preservation, may not give rise to disagreements which might compromise the amicable relations subsisting between the confederated states, all the members of the confederation must enter into a solemn engagement to devote their most serious attention to the superintendence which the present decree prescribes, and to exercise it in such a manner as to prevent as much as possible all reciprocal complaints and discussions.

Sect. 6.   In order, however, to assure better the guarantee of the moral and political inviolability of the states of the confederation, which is the object of the present decree, it is to be understood, that in case a government believe itself injured by writings published under another government, and cannot obtain complete satisfaction by amicable and diplomatic representations, that government will be at liberty to prefer its complaint to the Diet, which, in such a case, will hold itself bound to appoint a commission to examine the writing which shall have been thus denounced, and if the report of the commission state it to be necessary, to command the suppression of the said writing, and also to prohibit its continuance if it be of the number of periodical publications.

The Diet will proceed also, without a previous denunciation, and of its own authority, against every publication comprised in the principal regulation of Art. I. in whatever state of Germany it may be published, if in the opinion of a commission appointed to consider thereof, it may have compromised the dignity of the Germanic body, the safety of any of its members, or the internal peace of Germany, without any recourse being afforded against the judgment given in such a case, which shall be carried into execution by the government that is responsible for the condemned publication.

Sect. 7.   The editor of a journal, or other periodical publication, that may be suppressed by command of the Diet, shall not be allowed, during the space of five years, to conduct any similar publication in any states of the confederation.

The authors, editors and publishers of newspapers or periodical writings and others, mentioned in the first paragraph of Article 1, shall be, in other respects, upon submitting to the regulation of that article, free from all responsibility; and the judgments of the Diet, mentioned in the preceding article, will be directed only against the publications, without affecting individuals.

Sect. 8.   The confederated states engage within six months to acquaint the Diet with the measures which each shall have adopted to carry into execution the first article of this decree.

Sect. 9.   Every work printed in Germany, whether comprehended in the regulations of this decree or not, must bear the name of the printer or the editor; and if it be of the number of periodical publications, of the principal editor.   Every work in circulation in any of the states of the confederation, with respect to which these conditions have not been complied with, will be seized and confiscated, and the person or persons who may have published and sold it condemned, according to the circumstances of the case, to the payment of fine, or some other punishment proportionate to the offence.

Sect. 10.   The present decree shall remain in force during five years from the date of its publication.   Before the term of its expiration the Diet will take in to mature consideration in what manner the 18th article of the federal act relative to the uniformity of laws on the conduct of the press in the confederated states, can be carried into execution, by definitively fixing the legal limits of the press in Germany.

THE EMS DISPATCH, JULY 13, 1870

Bismarck had found a good issue on which he believed the French would go to war in the Hohenzollern-Sigmarigen candidacy for the Spanish throne. When information leaked in advance of the actual acceptance by the Cortes, the French indicated their anger. They finally were able to have the candidacy withdrawn, but went too far in demanding a promise that the King would never approve the candidacy in the future should it be renewed. The French Ambassador Benedetti went to the bathing Spa at Ems where he met William I and pressed the issue. The King finally informed him of the withdrawal of the candidacy, and ended the matter. Bismarck was distraught when he heard of this but saw his opportunity in the permission to announce what had occurred to the press. By careful editing of the statement he made it appear as though the French Ambassador was insulted. The French took up the issue and declared war.

    The original telegram and Bismarck's revision are included below.

Source: See German originals in Robert H. Lord, The Origins of the War of 1870. New Documents from the German Archives (New York: Russell & Russell, 1966), No. 163 (No. A 2301), pp. 220-221, and No. 187, pp. 231-232.

Original Telegram	Bismarck's Revision
Abeken to Bismarck	After the reports of the renunciation by the hereditary Prince of Hohenzollern had been officially transmitted by the Spanish Royal Government to the Imperial Government of France, the French Ambassador presented to His Majesty the King the demand to authorize him to telegraph Paris that His Majesty the King would obligate himself for all future time never again to give his approval to the Hohenzollern candidacy should it be renewed.
Ems, July 13, 1879	
His Majesty the King writes to me:	
"Count Benedetti intercepted me on the Promenade in order to demand of me most insistently that I should authorize him to telegraph immediately, that I shall obligate myself for all future time never again to give my approval to the Hohenzollern candidacy should it be renewed. I refused to agree to it, the last time somewhat severly, that one can not and dare not assume such obligations forever (à tout jamais). Naturally I told him, that I had not received news yet,	His Majesty therefore refused to see the French Ambassador again, and had so informed him through an adjutant that His Majesty had nothing further to say to the Ambassador.

and since he had been informed
earlier by way of Paris and Madrid,
he could easily understand that my
government was once again out of
the matter.''

His Majesty has since re-
ceived a dispatch from the Prince.
As His Majesty has told Count
Benedetti that he was expecting
news from the Prince, has in view
of the abovementioned demand and
in consonance with the advice of
Count Eulenberg and myself decided not to receive Count
Benedetti again, but to inform him
through an adjutant that His
Majesty had now received from the
Prince confirmation of the news
which Benedetti had already received from Paris, and that he had
nothing further to say to the
Ambassador.

His Majesty leaves it to Your
Exellency's judgement whether or
not to communicate at once Benedetti's new demand and its
rejection to our Ambassadors and
the Press.

ROYAL PROCLAMATION

CREATION OF THE EMPIRE, January 18, 1871

> Bismarck had worked hard for several years to achieve his
> goal of German unification. The Empire was officially pro-
> claimed on January 18, 1871 from the Versailles Palace outside
> of Paris. He was convinced that once the South German states
> fought along side their fellow Germans of the North German Con-
> federation they would be willing to unite in the new Empire. He
> had already prepared the way by a series of treaties.

Source: The Annual Register, 1871 (London, 1872), pp. 220-221.

Royal Proclamation read to the Upper and Lower Houses of the
Prussian Diet, January 18, announcing revival of the ancient title of
Emperor of Germany in the person of the Prussian monarch, now absent
at the siege of Paris.

We, William, by God's grace, King of Prussia, hereby announced
that the German Princes and Free Towns having addressed to us a unani-
mous call to renew and undertake with the reestablishment of the German
Empire the dignity of Emperor, which now for 60 years has been in obey-
ance, and the requisite provisions having been inserted in the constitution
of the German Confederation, we regard it as a duty we owe to the entire
Father and to comply with this call of the United German Princes, and to
accept the dignity of Emperor.

Accordingly, we and our successors to the Crown of Prussia hence-
forth shall use the Imperial title in all our relations and affairs of the
German Empire, and we hope to God that it may be vouchsafed to the
German nation to lead the Fatherland on to a blessed future under the aus-
pices of its ancient splendor. We undertake the Imperial dignity, conscious
of the duty to protect with German loyalty the rights of the Empire and its
members, to preserve peace, to maintain the independence of Germany, and
to strengthen the power of the people. We accept it in the hope that it will
be granted to the German people to enjoy it in lasting peace the reward of
its arduous and heroic struggles within boundaries which will give to the
Fatherland that security against renewed French attacks which it has
lacked for centuries.

May God grant to us and to our successors to the Imperial Crown,
that we may be the defenders of the German Empire at all times, not in
martial conquest, but in works of peace in the sphere of national prosperity, freedom, and civilizations.

CONSTITUTION OF THE GERMAN EMPIRE

April 16, 1871

The Empire was to a great extent Bismarck's creation. He was careful to create a constitutional framework which would please William I as Emperor and yet give him (Bismarck) and his successors as Chancellor enough power to maintain and control the nation. The various states were permitted to retain certain privileges.

Source: Great Britain, British and Foreign State Papers, 1870-1871 (London: William Ridgway, 1877), vol. LXI, pp. 58-76.

II. Legislature of the Empire.

II. Within this confederate territory the Empire exercises the right of legislation according to the tenor of this Constitution, and with the effect take the Imperial laws take precedence of the laws of the States. . . .

III. For entire Germany one common nationality exists with the effect, that every person (subject, State-citizen) belonging to any one of the Confederated States is to be treated in every other of the Confederated States as a born native. . . .

What is needful for the fulfilment of military duty in regard to the native country will be ordered by the way of Imperial legislation.

Every German has the same claim to the protection of the Empire with regard to foreign nations. . . .

V. The Legislation of the Empire is carried on by the council of the Confederation and the Imperial Diet. The accordance of the majority of votes in both Assemblies is necessary and sufficient for a law of the Empire. . . .

III. The Bundesrat

VI. The Bundesrat consists of the members of the confederation. . .

IV. The Presidency.

XI. The Presidency of the Reich belongs to the King of Prussia, who bears the name of German Emperor. The Emperor has to represent the Empire internationally, to declare war, and to conclude peace in the name of the Empire, to enter into alliances and other Treaties with Foreign Powers, to accredit and to receive Ambassadors.

The consent of the Bundesrat is necessary for the declaration of war in the name of the Empire, unless an attack on the territory or the coast of the Confederation has taken place . . .

XII.   The Emperor has the right to summon, to open, to prorogue, and to close both the Bundesrat and the Reichstag.

XIII.   The summoning of the Council of the Confederation, and of the Imperial Diet, takes place once each year. . . .

V.   Reichstag

XX.   The Imperial Diet is elected by universal and direct election with secret votes . . . .

XXIII.   The Reichstag has the right to propose laws within the competency of the Empire, and to forward Petitions which have been addressed to it to the Council of the Confederation, or to the Chancellor of the Empire.

XXVIII.   The Reichstag decides by absolute majority of votes.   The presence of a majority of the legal number of the members is necessary for the validity of a resolution. . . .

XXIX.   The members of the Reichstag are Representatives of the entire people, and are not bound by orders and instructions.

XXX.   No member of the Reichstag can at any time be proceeded against either judicially or by way of discipline, on account of his votes, or for expressions made use of in the exercise of his functions, nor can he be made responsible in any other way out of the Assembly . . . .

VI.   Customs and Commercial Affairs.

XXXIII.   Germany forms one customs and commercial territory encircled by a common customs frontier.   Those separate parts of territory are excluded, which from their position are not adapted for inclusion in the customs frontier. . . .

LVII.   Every German is liable to military service, and cannot have that service performed by substitute . . . .

THREE EMPERORS' LEAGUE, June 18, 1881

Bismarck had been concerned since the end of the Franco-
Prussian War that France would seek an alliance with some
nation such as Russia, and then create an atmosphere in which
Germany would be faced with a two-front war. Therefore the
German Chancellor had been working since the earlier arrangements of 1872-73 to arrange this alliance as a guarantee that
there would be neither a war between Austria and Russia nor a
Franco-Russian alliance. Each nation promised to remain neutral
if the others went to war. In addition the powers agreed to maintain the territorial status quo in Turkey. Bismarck considered
this treaty so important and secret that he personally conducted
the negotiations.

Source: Johannes Lepsius, Albrecht Mendelssohn Bartholdy, and Friedrich Thimme, eds. Die Grosse Politik (Berlin, 1922), vol. 3, no. 532,
pp. 176-179.

The Courts of Germany, Austria-Hungary and Russia, animated by an
equal desire to consolidate the general peace by an understanding destined
to assume the defensive position of their respective States, have come to an
agreement on certain questions which apply most specifically to their reciprocal interests.
(There follows the naming of the representatives).

Art. I. In case one of the High Contracting Parties should find itself
at war with a fourth Great Power, the two others shall maintain a benevolent
neutrality toward it and shall devote their efforts to the localization of the
conflict.
This stipulation shall apply equally to a war between one of the
three Powers and Turkey, but only in the case where a previous agreement
shall have been reached between the three Courts as to the result of this
war.
In the special case where one of them shall obtain a more positive
support from one of its two allies, the obligatory value of the present
Article shall remain in all its force for the third.
Art. II. Russia in agreement with Germany declares her firm resolution to respect the interests arising from the new position assumed to
Austria-Hungary by the Treaty of Berlin.
The three Courts desirous of avoiding all discord among them engage
to take account of their respective interests in the Balkan Peninsula. They
further promise that any new modification in the status quo of Turkey in
Europe can only be accomplished by virtue of common agreement among
them.
In order to facilitate the agreement contemplated by the present
Article, an agreement it is impossible to forsee all conditions, the three

Courts from the present record in the Protocol annexed to this Treaty on which an agreement has already been reestablished in principle.

Art. III. The three Courts recognize the European and mutually obligatory character of the principle of closing the Straits of the Bosphorud and of the Dardanelles, founded an international law, confirmed by treaties . . . .

They will take care in common that Turkey shall make no exception in their rule in favor of the interests of any government whatsoever, by lending to guerilla operations of a belligerent Power the portion of its empire constituted by the Straits.

In case of infringement or in order to prevent it if such infringement should be in prospect, the three Courts will inform Turkey that they consider her in that event as putting herself in a state of war toward the injured party, and as having deprived herself thenceforth of the benefits of the security assured to her territorial status quo by the Treaty of Berlin.

Art. IV. The present Treaty shall be in force during a period of three years from the day of exchange of ratifications.

Art. V. The High Contracting Parties mutually promise secrecy on the contents and the existence of the present Treaty, as well of the Protocol thereto.

Art. VI. The secret conventions concluded between Germany and Russia and between Austria-Hungary and Russia in 1873 are replaced by the present Treaty.

In witness thereof the respective Plenipotentiaries have signed the present Treaty and have affixed thereto the seal of their arms.

Done at Berlin the eighteenth day of the month of June of the year one thousand eight hundred and eighty-one.

(L. S.) v. Bismarck
(L. S.) Szechenyi
(L. S.) Sabouroff

ATTACHED PROTOCOL OF THE THREE EMPERORS' LEAGUE

The undersigned Plenipotentiaries of [the three monarchs] . . . having established conformity to Article II of the secret Treaty concluded today the points touching the interests of the three Courts of Germany, Austria-Hungary and Russia in the Balkan Peninsula with whom an agreement has already been established among them have agreed on the following Protocol:

1. Bosnia and Herzegovinia
   Austria-Hungary reserves the right to annex these two provinces at whatever moment she shall deem opportune.

3. Eastern Rumelia
   The three Powers agree in regarding the eventuality of an occupation either of Eastern Rumelia or of the Balkans as full of perils for the general peace. In case this should occur they will employ their efforts to

dissuade the Porte from such an enterprise, it being well understood that Bulgaria and Eastern Rumelia on their part are to abstain from provoking the Port by attacks coming from their territories against the other provinces of the Ottoman Empire.

4. Bulgaria
       The three Powers will not oppose the eventual reunion of Bulgaria and Eastern Bulgaria within the territorial limits which have been assigned to them by the Treaty of Berlin, if this question should come up by the force of circumstances. They agree to dissuade the Bulgarians from all aggression against the neighboring provinces, particularly Macedonia and to explain them that in such a case they will act at their own risk and peril.

6. The present Protocol forms an integral part of the secret Treaty signed on this day in Berlin and will have the same force and validity.

       Done at Berlin, the 18th June 1881.

                                        (L. S.) v. Bismarck
                                        (L. S.) Szechenyi
                                        (L. S.) Sabouroff

TRIPLE ALLIANCE, May 20, 1882

Bismarck took advantage of Italy's distress over French seizure
of Tunisia to expand the Dual Alliance into the Triple Alliance.
Italy had needed French aid in her struggle for unity against
Austria and so she again needed powerful allies to achieve her
territorial goals in Africa. She also was concerned that France
might attempt to restore the temporal power of the papacy. The
three powers agreed to consult with each other in case one is
attacked so that they might plan any possible military cooperation.

Source: Johannes Lepsius, Albrecht Mendelssohn Bartholdy, and Friedrich Thimme, eds.   Die Grosse Politik (Berlin, 1922), vol. 3, No. 571,
pp. 245-247.

Their Majesties the Emperor of Germany, King of Prussia, the Emperor of Austria, King of Bohemia, etc. and Apostolic King of Hungary and
the King of Italy animated by the desire to augment the guarantees of the
general peace, to strengthen the monarchical principal and to assure that
the same maintains the social and political order in their respective states
have agreed to conclude a Treaty which, by its essentially conservative and
defensive nature only pursue the goal of forewarning them against the
dangers which would threaten the security of their States and the peace of
Europe.

For this effect their majesties have named [Plenipotentiares named]
who furnished with full powers ... have agreed upon the following articles:

Art. I. The High Contracting Parties mutually promise peace and
friendship, and will enter into no alliance or engagement directed against
any one of their States.

They engage to proceed to an exchange of ideas on the political and
economic questions of a general nature which may arise, and promise as
another their mutual support within the limits of their own interests.

Art. II.   In case Italy, without direct provocation on her part, should
be attacked by France for any reason whatsoever, the two other contracting Parties shall be bound to lend help and assistance with all their
forces to the party attacked.

The same obligation shall be incumbent on Italy in case of any
aggression without direct provocation of France against Germany.

Art. III.   If one, or two, of the high contracting Parties, without
direct provocation on their part, should chance to be attacked and to be
engaged in a war with two or more Great Powers nonsignatory to the
present Treaty the causus foederis will arise simultaneously for all the
high contracting Parties.

Art. IV. In case a Great Power non-signatory to the present treaty should threaten the security of the states of one of the high contracting Parties and the threatened party should find itself forced to make war against it, the two others bind themselves to observe toward their ally, a benevolent neutrality. Each of them reserves to itself in this case the right to take part in the war, if it should see fit to make common cause with its ally.

Art. V. If the peace of one of the high contracting Parties should chance to be threatened under the circumstances foreseen by the preceding articles the high contracting Parties shall take counsel together in ample time on the military measures to be taken with a view toward eventual cooperation.

They engage henceforward, in all cases of common participation in a war, to conclude neither armistice, nor peace, nor treaty except by common agreement among them.

Art. VI. The high contracting Parties mutually promise secrecy as to the contents and existence of the Present Treaty.

Art. VII. The present Treaty will remain in force during the space of five years dating from the day of the exchange of ratifications.

Done at Vienna, the twentieth day of the month of May of the year one thousand eight hundred eighty-two.

> (L. S.) Henri VII Prince of Reuss
> (Germany)
> (L. S.) Gustave Kalnoky
> (Austria-Hungary)
> (L. S.) Charles de Robilant (Italy)

REINSURANCE TREATY, June 18, 1887

Bismarck was still concerned with the isolation of France. Russia had refused to renew the Three Emperors' League in 1887 because the Congress of Berlin had forced her to return almost all the territory she had taken from Turkey at the end of the Russo-Turkish War. This Treaty was evidence of Bismarck's diplomatic skills in which he now had a treaty against Austria as well as the earlier Dual Alliance against Russia.

Source: Johannes Lepsius, Albrecht Mendelssohn Bartholdy, and Friedrich Thimme, eds.   Die Grosse Politik (Berlin, 1922), vol. 5, No. 1092, pp. 253-255.)

The Imperial Courts of Germany and of Russia animated by an equal desire to strengthen the general peace by an entente destined to assure the defensive position of their respective States, have resolved to consecrate by a special arrangement the agreement established between them in view of the expiration on June 15/27, in 1881 and renewed in 1884 by the three courts of Germany, Russia, and Austria-Hungary.

To this effect the two Courts have named. . . . Plenipotentiaries . . . who . . . have agreed upon the following articles.

Art. I. In case one of the high contracting Parties should find itself at war with a third Great Power, the other would maintain a benevolent neutrality towards it and would devote its efforts to the localization of the conflict. This deposition should not be applied in a war against Austria or France in the case where this war should result in an attack directed against one of the two latter powers by one of the high contracting parties.

Art. II. Germany recognizes the historic rights acquired by Russia in the Balkan Peninsula and particularly the legitimacy of its preponderant and decisive influence in Bulgaria and Eastern Rumelia. The two Courts engage themselves to admit no modification of the territorial status quo of the said peninsula without a previous agreement between them, and to oppose, when occasion arises, every attempt to disturb this status quo or to modify it without their consent.

Art. III. The two Courts recognize the European and mutually obligatory character of the principal of the closing of the straits of the Bosphorus and of the Dardanelles founded on international law, confirmed by treaties . . .

They will take care in common that Turkey shall make no exception to this rule in favor of the interest of any Government whatsoever by lending to warlike operations of a belligerent power the portion of its Empire which constitute the Straits.

In case of infringement or to prevent it if an infraction should be in prospect, the two Courts will inform Turkey that they would regard her, in that case, as putting her in a state of war toward the injured party, and as depriving herself of the benefits of security assured to her the territorial status quo by the Treaty of Berlin.

Art. IV.   The present treaty shall remain in force for the space of three years dating from the exchange of ratifications.

Done at Berlin, the eighteenth day of the month of July one thousand eight hundred and eighty-seven.

> (L. S.) Count Bismarck
> (L. S.) Count Paul Schouvaloff

ADDITIONAL AND MOST SECRET PROTOCOL

In order to complete the stipulations of Articles II and III of the secret treaty on this same date, the two Courts have come to an agreement on the following points.

1.   Germany, as in the past, will lend its assistance to Russia in order to reestablish a regular and legal government in Bulgaria.--She promises in no case to give her consent to the restoration of the Prince of Battenberg.

2.   In case His Majesty the Emperor of Russia should find himself under the necessity of assuming the task of defending the entrance of the Black Sea in order to safeguard the interests of Russia, Germany engages to accord her benevolent neutrality and her moral and diplomatic support to the measures which His Majesty may judge necessary to take to guard the key of this Empire.

Done at Berlin, the eighteenth day of the month of July one thousand eight hundred and eighty-seven.

> (L.S.) Count Bismarck
> (L.S.) Count Paul Schouvaloff

KRUGER TELEGRAM, January 3, 1896

In this message William II gave evidence of his desire to offer support to the South African Boers in their struggle against Britain.

Source: E. T. S. Dugdale, ed. and trans., German Diplomatic Documents, 1871-1914, (New York: Harper & Brothers, 1929), vol. II, 1. 387.

January 3rd, 1896

The Emperor William to President Kruger, Drafted by Kayser of the Foreign Office (Colonial Section)

(Sent off at 11:20 A. M.)

I express my sincere congratulations that, supported by your people, without appealing for the help of friendly Powers, you have succeeded by your own energetic action against armed bands which invaded your country as disturbers of the peace, and thus have been enabled to restore peace and safeguard the independence of the country against attacks from the outside.

William I. R.

THE BLANK CHECK, July 16, 1914

Germany's guarantee to back Austria-Hungary in whatever
decision she made in regard to her demands on Serbia helped
to turn the scales toward the war party in the Imperial Cabinet.
The government was thus encouraged to go ahead with its plans
to deliver the demand for Serbian capitulation.

Source: Max Montegelas and Walther Schucking, eds. Outbreak of the
World War. German Documents Collected by Karl Kautsky. Trans. by
the Carnegie Endowment for International Peace. Division of International
Law (New York: Oxford University Press, 1924), pp. 78-79.

Confidential.   For Your Excellency's personal information and guid-
ance.   Berlin, July 6, 1914.

The Austro-Hungarian Ambassador yesterday delivered to the Emperor a confidential personal letter from the Emperor Franz Joseph, which
depicts the present situation from the Austro-Hungarian point of view, and
describes the measures which Vienna has in view. A copy is now being
forwarded to Your Excellency.

I replied to Count Szogyeny today on behalf of His Majesty that His
Majesty sends his thanks to the Emperor Franz Joseph for his letter and
would soon answer it personally. In the meantime His Majesty desires
to say that he is not blind to the danger which threatens Austria-Hungary
and thus the Triple Alliance as a result of the Russian and Serbian Pan-
slavic agitation. Even though His Majesty is known to feel no unqualified
confidence in Bulgaria and her ruler, and naturally inclines more toward
our old ally Roumania and her Hohenzollern prince, yet he quite under-
stands that the Emperor Franz Joseph, in view of the attitude of Roumania
and of the danger of a new Balkan alliance aimed directly at the Danube
Monarchy, is anxious to bring about an understanding between Bulgaria and
the Triple Alliance. His Majesty will, furthermore, make an effort at
Bucharest, according to the wishes of the Emperor Franz Joseph, to influence King Carol to the fulfilment of the duties of his alliance, to the
renunciation of Serbia, and to the suppression of the Roumanian agitations
directed against Austria-Hungary.

Finally, as far as concerns Serbia, His Majesty, of course, can not
interfere in the dispute now going on between Austria-Hungary and that
country, as it is a matter not within his competence. The Emperor Franz
Joseph may, however, rest assured that His Majesty will faithfully stand
by Austria-Hungary, as is required by the obligations of his alliance and
of his ancient friendship.

Bethmann-Hollweg.

ZIMMERMANN TELEGRAM, January 19, 1917

German Foreign Secretary Arthur Zimmermann informed the German Ambassador about the intention of the government to resume unrestricted submarine warfare in the hope that the United States could be convinced to remain neutral. If this were not possible then the Mexicans were to be encouraged to declare war against their northern neighbor. This note was intercepted by the British and delivered to the American Ambassador, Walter Hines Page. The knowledge of this proposal aroused anti-German sentiment in the United States.

Source: <u>Congressional</u> <u>Record</u>, vol. LIV: P.4596, March 1, 1917.

Berlin, January 19, 1917

On the first of February, we intend to begin submarine warfare unrestricted. In spite of this, it is our intention to endeavor to keep neutral the United States of America.

If this is not successful we propose an alliance on the following basis with Mexico: That we shall make war together, and it is understood that Mexico is to reconquer the lost territory in New Mexico, Texas and Arizona. The details are left to you for settlement.

You are instructed to inform the President of Mexico of the above in the greatest confidence as soon as it is certain that there will be an outbreak of war with the United States and suggest that the President of Mexico, on his own initiative, should communicate with Japan suggesting adherence at once to this plan; at the same time, offer to mediate between Germany and Japan.

Please call to the attention of the President of Mexico that the employment of ruthless submarine warfare now promises to compel England to make peace in a few months.

Zimmermann

VERSAILLES PEACE TREATY, June 28, 1919

Germany was forced to surrender unconditionally and to accept
the peace dictated by the Allied Powers. She and her allies were
to take full responsibility for the war. Germany's armed forces
were severly limited in size as well as length and condition of
service. In addition she was not to have any airforce. Finally,
Germany was to accept the concept of reparations payments for
damages caused to the civilian population during the war. The
amount was to be determined by a Reparations Commission in
the future.

Source: The Treaty of Peace Between the Allied and Associated Powers
and Germany. Signed at Versailles, 28th June 1919. (London: Printed and
Published by His Majesty's Stationery Office, 1919.)

Part VIII. Reparation

Section I. General Provisions

Article 231. The Allied and Associated Governments affirm and
Germany accepts the responsibility of Germany and her allies for causing
all the loss and damage to which the Allied and Associated Governments
and their nationals have been subjected as a consequence of the war
imposed upon them by the aggression of Germany and her allies.
Article 232 . . .
The Allied and Associated Governments, however, require, and
Germany undertakes, that she will make compensation for all damage
done to the civilian population of the Allied and Associated Powers and
to their property during the period of belligerency of each as an Allied
or Associate Power, against Germany by such aggression by land, by
sea and from the air. . . .
Article 233.   The amount of the above damage for which com-
pensation is to be made by Germany shall be determined by an Inter-
Allied Commission, to be called the Reparation Commission. . . .
The Commission shall consider the claims and give to the German
Government a just opportunity to be heard.

WEIMAR CONSTITUTION, August 11, 1919

The Germans were encouraged to consolidate and stabilize their
position after their defeat in the First World War and the abdication of the Kaiser. A National Constituent Assembly, elected
January 19, 1919, met at Weimar on February 19, concluded its
work on July 31. The Constitution went into effect on August 11.
The Assembly had attempted to take the best features of the
various Bills of Rights as established in France, Britain and
the United States. But the Weimar Republic came into existence
having to carry the onerous burden of the Versailles Peace
Settlement. The extracts show the various important points of
the Constitution, especially Article 48 which gave the President
of the Reich emergency powers to be used in time of crisis.

Source: Frederick F. Blachly and Miriam E. Oatman. The Government
and Administration of Germany, Institute for Government Research of
the Brooklings Institution (Baltimore, Maryland: The Johns Hopkins Press,
1928), pp. 642-679.

The German people, united in its racial branches and animated
by the purpose of renewing and fortifying its Reich in freedom and justice,
of preserving domestic and foreign peace, and of promoting social progress, has adopted this Constitution.

DIVISION I

STRUCTURE AND FUNCTIONS OF THE REICH

CHAPTER I
REICH AND STATE

Article 1. The German Reich is a Republic. Supreme power emanates from the people.
   Art. 2.   The territory of the Reich consists of the territories of
the German states. Other territories can be received into the Reich by
means of a national law, if their inhabitants request this by virtue of the
right of self-determination.
   Art. 3.   The national colors are black, red and gold. The commercial flag is black, white, and red, with the national colors in the upper
inner corner.
   Art. 4.   The generally recognized rules of international law are
valid as binding portions of the German national law.
   Art. 5. Sovereignty is exercised in national affairs through organs
of the Reich on the basis of the national Constitution, in state affairs
through the organs of the states on the basis of the state Constitutions. . . .
   Art. 9.   In so far as a need exists for the issuing of uniform pro-

visions, the Reich has legislative power over:

    1. Public welfare.

    2. The protection of public order and safety. * * *

    Art. 12. So long and so far as the Reich does not make use of its legislative power, the states retain the right of legislation. This does not hold for the exclusive legislative power of the Reich. . . .

    Art. 13. National law overrules state law.

    If doubts or differences of opinion exist, as to whether a provision of state law is compatible with the national law, the appropriate national or state central authorities may request the decision of a supreme court of the Reich, according to the more detailed provisions of a national law. . . .

    Art. 16. The officers entrusted with direct national administration in the states as a rule shall be citizens of such states.

    Art. 17. Every state must have a republican Constitution. The popular representatives must be elected by the universal, equal, direct, and secret suffrage of all men and women who are citizens of the Reich, according to the fundamental principles of proportional representation. The state Cabinet must have the confidence of the representatives of the people.

    The fundamental principles for election to the popular house are also valid for the local elections. However, through state law the right of suffrage may be made dependent upon a period of residence in the commune up to one year.

    Art. 18. The division of the Reich into states shall serve the highest economic and cultural development of the people, with the utmost possible consideration of the will of the population affected. . . .

CHAPTER II

THE REICHSTAG

    Article 20. The Reichstag consists of the delegates of the German people.

    Art. 21. The delegates are representatives of the entire people. They are subject only to their consciences, and are not bound by instructions.

    Art. 22. The delegates are elected by universal, equal, direct, and secret suffrage of men and women over twenty years of age, according to the funamental principles of proportional representation. The election day must be a Sunday or a public holiday.

    The national election law prescribes the details.

    Art. 23. The Reichstag is elected for four yers. The new election must take place at the latest on the sixtieth day after the expiration of this period.

    The Reichstag assembles for the first time at the latest on the thirtieth day after the election. * * *

    Art. 25. The national President can dissolve the Reichstag, but only once for the same reason.

The new election takes place at the latest on the sixtieth day after the dissolution.

CHAPTER III

THE NATIONAL PRESIDENT AND THE NATIONAL CABINET

Article 41.   The national President is elected by the entire German people.

Any German is eligible who has completed the thirty-fifth year of his life.

The details are provided by a national law.

Art.   42.   Upon assuming office, the national President takes the following oath before the Reichstag:

I swear that I will devote my powers to the welfare of the German people, will develop its advantages, will guard it against dangers, will uphold the Constitution and the laws of the Reich, will fulfil my duties conscientiously, and will practice justice toward everyone.

The addition of a religious sanction is permissible.

Art. 43.   The national President holds office for seven years.   Re-election is permissible.

Before the completion of the term, the national President may be removed by popular vote, upon the motion of the Reichstag.   The decision of the Reichstag requires a two-thirds majority.   Through the decision the national President is suspended from the further exercise of his functions. . . .

Art.   48.   If a state does not fulfil the duties incumbent upon it according to the national Constitution or the national laws, the national President may compel it to do so with the aid of the armed forces.

If the public safety and order in the German Reich are seriously disturbed or endangered, the national President may take the measure necessary for the restoration of public safety and order, and may intervene if necessary with the assistance of the armed forces.   For this purpose he may temporarily set aside in whole or in part, the fundamental rights established in Articles 114, 115, 117, 118, 123, 124, and 153.

The national President must immediately inform the Reichstag of all measures taken in conformity with paragraph 1 or paragraph 2 of this Article.   The measures are to be revoked upon the demand of the Reichstag.

In case of imminent danger, the state government may take for its territory temporary measures of the nature described in paragraph 2. The measures are to be revoked upon the demand of the national President or of the Reichstag.

A national law shall prescribe the details. . . .

Art.   50.   All ordinances and orders of the national President, including those within the domain of the armed forces, require for their validity countersignature by the national Chancellor or the national minister concerned.   Through the countersignature responsibility is assumed. . . .

Art.   52.   The national Cabinet consists of the national Chancellor and the national ministers.

Art. 53. The national Chancellor, and upon his proposal the national ministers, are appointed and dismissed by the national President.

Art. 54. The national Chancellor and the national ministers require for the conduct of their offices the confidence of the Reichstag. Each of them must retire if the Reichstag withdraws its confidence from him by an express vote.

Art. 55. The national Chancellor presides over the Cabinet and conducts its business according to an order of business which is adopted by the national Cabinet with the consent of the national President.

Art. 56. The national Chancellor establishes the outlines of policy and bears the responsibility therefor in respect ot the Reichstag. . . .

CHAPTER IV

THE REICHSRAT

Article 60. A Reichsrat is established to represent the German states in the legislation and administration of the Reich.

Art. 61. In the Reichsrat every state has at least one vote. In the larger states one vote is given for each 700,000 inhabitants. A remainder of at least 350,000 inhabitants is counted as 700,000. No state may be represented by more than two-fifths of all the votes.* . . .

Art. 62. In the committees which the Reichsrat appoints from among its members, no state has more than one vote.

Art. 63. The states are represented in the Reichsrat through members of their cabinets. Half of the Prussian votes, however, are to be cast by the Prussian provincial administrations, according to the provisions of a state law.

The states are entitled to send as many representatives to the Reichsrat as they have votes.

* As amended by law of March 25, 1921.

CHAPTER V

NATIONAL LEGISLATION

Article 68. Proposals for laws are brought in by the national Cabinet or from the body of the Reichstag.

National laws are enacted by the Reichstag.

Art. 69. The bringing in of proposals for laws by the national Cabinet requires the consent of the Reichsrat. If an agreement is not reached between the national Cabinet and the Reichsrat, the national Cabinet may nevertheless bring in the proposal, but in so doing, must state the dissenting position of the Reichsrat. . . .

Art. 73. A law passed by the Reichstag is to be submitted to a popular referendum before its publication, if the national President so decides within one month. . . .

A popular referendum is also to be held if one-tenth of the qualified voters petition for the introduction of a bill. The popular petition must be based upon a completely drafted bill. . . .

Art. 76. The Constitution can be amended by way of legislation. . . . only if two-thirds of the legal membership (of the Reichstag and the Reichsrat) is present and at least two-thirds of those present vote in the affirmative.

CHAPTER VI

THE NATIONAL ADMINISTRATION

Article 78. The cultivation of relationships with foreign states is exclusively a function of the Reich.

The states may conclude treaties with foreign countries, in respect to matters the regulation of which falls within the state legislative power; these treaties require the consent of the Reich.

Agreements with foreign powers in respect to changes in national boundaries are made by the Reich with the consent of the state affected. Changes in boundaries may take place only on the basis of a national law, except where a mere correction of the boundarie of uninhabited regions is concerned.

In order to assure the representation of interests arising from the special economic relationships or the geographical proximity of individual states in respect to foreign countries, the Reich decides upon the requisite arrangements and measures in agreement with the states concerned. . . .

DIVISION II

FUNDAMENTAL RIGHTS AND DUTIES OF GERMANS

CHAPTER I

THE INDIVIDUAL PERSON

Article 109. All Germans are equal before the law.

Men and women have fundamentally the same civil rights and duties.

Public-legal privileges or disadvantages of birth or of rank are abolished. Titles of nobility are considered only as a part of the name, and may no longer be bestowed. . . .

Art. 110. Citizenship in the Reich and in the states is acquired and lost according to the provisions of a national law. Every citizen of a state is at the same time a citizen of the Reich. . . .

Art. 111. All Germans enjoy freedom of travel and residence throughout the Reich. . . .

Art. 112. Every German has the right to emigrate to foreign countries. Emigration can be limited only by national law. . . .

Art. 114. The freedom of the person is inviolable. Any limitation or encroachment upon personal freedom by public authority is permissible only upon a statutory basis.

Persons deprived of freedom are to be informed at latest on the following day by what authority and on what grounds the deprivation of their freedom was ordered; they shall immediately be given an opportunity to take measures opposing the loss of their freedom.

Art. 115. The dwelling of every German is for him a sanctuary and inviolable. Exceptions are permissible only on the basis of law.

Art. 116. An act can involve a penalty only if the penalty was fixed by law before the act was committed.

Art. 117. Secrecy of correspondence, as well as secrecy of the post, the telegraph, and the telephone, are inviolable. Exceptions can be permitted only by national law.

Art. 118. Within the limits of the general laws, every German has the right to express his opinion freely in words, writing, print, pictures, or in other ways. . . .

CHAPTER II

SOCIAL RELATIONS

Article 119. Marriage, as the foundation of family life and of the maintenance and the increase of the nation, stands under the especial protection of the Constitution. It rests upon the equal rights of the two sexes.

To foster the purity, soundness, and social progress of the family is a funtion of the states and of the communes. Families with many children have a right to claim the protection and care of the state.

Motherhood has a right to claim the protection and care of the state.

Art. 120. To educate the rising generation in physical, mental, and social fitness is the highest duty and the natural right of parents, whose activity is supervised by the political community.

Art. 122. Youth is to be protected against exploitation and against moral, mental, or physical neglect. State and communes must take the necessary measures. . . .

Art. 123. All Germans have the right to assemble peaceably and unarmed without notice or special permission. . . .

Art. 124. All Germans have the right to form associations or organizations for purposes which do not contravene the criminal laws. . . .

Art. 125. Freedom of election and secrecy of election are guaranteed. The details are provided by the election laws. . . .

CHAPTER III

RELIGION AND RELIGIOUS BODIES

Art. 135. All inhabitants of the Reich enjoy full religious freedom and freedom of conscience. The free exercise of religion is guaranteed by the constitution and is under public protection.

DOCUMENTS

127

Art. 137. There is no State Church.
Freedom of association is guaranteed to religious bodies. ...

CHAPTER IV

EDUCATION AND SCHOOLS

Article 142. Art, science, and the teaching of the same are free. The state guarantees their protection and participates in their cultivation.
Art. 143. Provision for the education of the young is to be made through public institutions. ...

CHAPTER V

THE ECONOMIC LIFE

Article 151. The ordering of the economic life must correspond to the fundamental principles of justice, with the purpose of guaranteeing to everyone an existence worthy of mankind. Within these limits the economic freedom of the individual is to be safeguarded. ...
Freedom of commerce and of industry is guaranteed in accordance with provisions of the national laws.
Art. 152. In economic intercourse, freedom of contract prevails in accordance with the provisions of the laws.
Usury is forbidden. ...
Art. 153. Property is guaranteed by the Constitution. Its content and its limitations are defined by the laws.
Expropriation can take place only for the general welfare, and upon statutory grounds. ...
Art. 157. The forces of labor stand under the especial protection of the Reich.
The Reich is to adopt a uniform labor law.
Art. 158. Intellectual labor, the rights of authors, inventors, and artists enjoy the protection and care of the Reich. ...
Art. 159. Freedom of association in order to protect and develop conditions of labor and economics life is guaranteed for everyone and for all occupations. ...
Art. 161. The Reich establishes a comprehensive insurance system, with the dominant cooperation of the insured, in order to maintain health and working capacity, to protect motherhood, and to provide against the economic consequences of old age, infirmity, and the vicissitudes of life. ...
Art. 164. The independent middle class in agriculture, industry, and commerce, is to be assisted by law and administration and guaranteed against oppression and destruction.
Art. 165. Laborers and employees are to cooperate on equal terms in association with entrepeneurs, in the regulation of conditions of wages and labor, as well as in the entire economic development of the productive forces. The organizations of both sides, and their agreements, are recognized. ...

TRANSITIONAL AND FINAL PROVISIONS

Art. 180. Until the first Reichstag assembles, the National Assembly serves as Reichstag. Until the first national President takes office, his functions are carried on by the national President elected on the basis of the law on the provisional national authority. *

Art. 181. The German people, through its National Assembly, has adopted and established this constitution. It goes into effect on the day of publication.

* The second sentence of Art. 180 was replaced through a law of Oct. 27, 1922, by the following sentence: The national President elected by the national Assembly holds office until June 30, 1925.

NAZI PARTY PROGRAM: TWENTY-FIVE POINTS

This program developed for the Party and proclaimed on February 25, 1920, was symbolic of its determination to appeal to all segments of the German population. Among other issues it condemned the Versailles Treaty, promised justice, protection of labor, and religious freedom (except for the Jews).

Source: Henri Lichtenberger. The Third Reich, Trans from French and edited by Koppel S. Pinson (New York: The Greystone Press, 1937), pp. 301-303.

The Program of the German Workers' Party is a program for the times. The leaders have no intention, once the aims announced in it have been achieved, of setting up new ones, merely in order to ensure the continued existence of the party through artificially stimulated discontent of the masses.

1. We demand the union of all Germans to form a Great Germany on the basis of the right of self-determination of nations.

2. We demand the equality of Germany with other nations, and the abolition of the Peace Treaties of Versailles and Saint-Germain.

3. We demand land and territory (colonies) for the sustenance of our people and for settling our superfluous population.

4. None but members of the nationality may be citizens of the state. None but those of German blood, irrespective of religion, may be members of the nationality. No Jew, therefore, is a member of the nationality.

5. Anyone who is not a citizen of the state may live in Germany only as a guest and must be subject to the law for aliens.

6. The right to determine the leadership and laws of the state is to be enjoyed only by citizens of the state. We demand, therefore, that all public offices, of whatever kind, whether in the Reich, in the states, or in the municipalities, shall be filled only by citizens of the state. We oppose the corrupt parliamentary system of filling posts merely with a view to party considerations and without reference to character or ability.

7. We demand that the state shall make its first duty to promote the industry and the livelihood of the citizens of the state. If it is not possible to maintain the entire population of the state then the members of foreign nations (non-citizens) must be expelled from the Reich.

8. All further immigration of non-Germans must be prevented. We demand that all non-Germans who entered Germany subsequent to August 2, 1914, shall be forced to leave the Reich forthwith.

9. All citizens shall enjoy equal rights and duties.

10. The primary duty of every citizen is to work either intellectually or physically. The activities of the individual must not clash with the interests of the community but must be realized within the frame of the whole

and to the advantage of all.

We therefore demand:

11. Abolition of incomes unearned by either work or effort.

Breaking of the Bonds of Interest Slavery

12. In view of the enormous sacrifices of property and life demanded of a people in every war, personal enrichment through war must be regarded as a crime against the nation. We demand, therefore, ruthless confiscation of all war profits.

13. We demand nationalization of all trusts.

14. We demand profit sharing in large concerns.

15. We demand the extensive development of old age pensions.

16. We demand the creation and maintenance of a healthy middle class, immediate communalization of department stores, and their lease at cheap rates to small merchants and extreme consideration for all small merchants in purchases by the federal government, states and municipalities.

17. We demand land reform adapted to our natonal needs, the enactment of a law for confiscation without compensation of land for public purposes; abolition of land interest and prevention of all speculation in land.

18. We demand a most ruthless struggle against those whose activities are injurious to the public interest. Base crimes against the nation, usurers, profiteers, etc., irrespective of creed or race, must be punished with death.

19. We demand the substitution of a German common law for the materialistic cosmopolitan Roman law.

20. In order to make it possible for every talented and diligent German to acquire a higher education and thus be able to occupy leading positions, the state must carry out a thorough reconstruction of our entire educational system. The curricula of all educational institutions must be adapted to the needs of practical life. The comprehension of political ideas, from the beginning of a child's understanding, must be the goal of the school (through civic education). We demand the education of intellectually gifted children of poor parents without regard to class or occupation, and at the expense of the state.

21. The state must take care of improvement in public health through protection of mothers and children, through prohibiting child labor, through increasing physical development by obligatory gymnastics and sports laid down by law, and by the extensive support of all organizations concerned with the physical development of young people.

22. We demand the abolition of mercenary troops and the formation of a national army.

23. We demand a legal battle against deliberate political lies and their dissemination by the press. In order to make possible the creation of a German press we demand:

    (a) All editors and contributors of newspapers appearing in the German language must be members of the German nationality.

    (b) Non-German newspapers must require express permission

of the state before they appear.   They must not be printed in
the German language.

(c) Non-Germans must be forbidden by law to participate fi-
nancially in German newspapers or to influence them. As punishment for violation of this law we demand that such a newspaper
be immediately suppressed and the non-German participating in
it be immediately expelled from the country. Newspapers which
give offense to the national welfare must be suppressed. We
demand legal battle against any tendency in art and literature
which exercises a disintegrating influence on our national life.
Institutions which violate the above mentioned demands must
be shut down.

24.   We demand liberty for all religious confessions in the state
in so far as they do not in any way endanger its existence or do not
offend the moral sentiment and the customs of the Germanic race. The
party as such represents the standpoint of positive Christianity without
binding itself confessionally to a particular faith. It opposes the Jewish
materialistic spirit within and without and is convinced that permanent
recovery of our people is possible only from within and on the basis
of the principle of:

General Welfare Before Individual Welfare

25.   In order to carry out all these demands we call for the creation
of a strong central authority in the Reich with unconditional authority
by the political central parliament over the entire Reich and all its organizations, and the formation of chambers of classes and occupations
to carry out the laws promulgated by the Reich in the various individual
states of the federation. The leaders of the party promise that they will
fight for the realization of the above mentioned points and if necessary
even sacrifice their lives.

Munich, February 24, 1920.

After due consideration the general membership of the party decided on May 22, 1926 that "This program is never to be changed."

NUREMBERG LAWS, September 15, 1935

The Nazi Party was determined to reduce and eliminate all power
and influence of the Jews in Germany. Racial purity was the aim
of the Party. Jews had been attacked even before the Party came
to power. They used the various governmental agencies to eliminate Jews from all aspects of German life.

Source: Henri Lichtenberger. The Third Reich. Trans. from French
and edited by Koppel S. Pinson (New York: The Greystone Press, 1937),
pp. 312-315.

I. THE REICH CITIZENSHIP LAW of September 15, 1935

The Reichstag has adopted unanimously the following law which is here-
with promulgated.

Article 1

(1) A subject of the state is he who belongs to the protective union of
the German Reich and who, therefore, has particular obligations towards
the Reich.

(2) The status of subject is acquired in accordance with the provisions of the Reich and State Law of Citizenship.

Article 2

(1) A citizen of the Reich is only that subject who is of German or
kindred blood and who, through his conduct, shows that he is both desirous and fit to serve faithfully the German people and the Reich.

(2) The right to citizenship is acquired by the granting of Reich citizenship papers.

(3) Only the citizen of the Reich enjoys full political rights in accordance with the provisions of the laws.

Article 3

The Reich Minister of the Interior in conjunction with the Deputy to
the Fuhrer will issue the necessary legal and administrative decrees for
the carrying out and amplification of this law.

Promulgated: September 16, 1935. In force: September 30, 1935.

I a.   FIRST SUPPLEMENTARY DECREE OF NOVEMBER 14, 1935

On the basis of Article 3 of the Reich Law of Citizenship of September 15, 1935, the following is hereby decreed:

Article 1

(1) Until further provisions regarding citizenship papers all subjects of German or kindred blood who possessed the right to vote in the Reichstag elections at the time the Law of Citizenship came into effect shall for the time being possess the rights of Reich citizens. The same shall be true of those upon whom the Reich Minister of Interior in conjunction with the Deputy to the Führer shall bestow citizenship.

(2) The Reich Minister of the Interior, in conjunction with the Deputy to the Führer may revoke citizenship.

Article 2

(1) The provisions of Article 1 apply also to subjects who are of mixed Jewish blood.

(2) An individual of mixed Jewish blood is one who is descended from one or two grandparents who were racially full Jews, in so far as he does not count as a Jew according to Section 2 of Article 5. As full-blooded Jewish grandparents shall be considered those who belonged to the Jewish religious community.

Article 3

Only citizens of the Reich, as bearers of full political rights, can exercise the right of voting in political affairs, and can hold public office. The Reich Minister of the Interior or any agency empowered by him can make exceptions during the transition period with regard to occupying public office. These measures do not apply to affairs pertaining to religious organizations.

Article 4

(1) A Jew cannot be a citizen of the Reich. He cannot exercise the right to vote; he cannot occupy public office.

(2) Jewish officials are to be retired as of December 31, 1935. In case these officials served at the front in the World War, either for Germany or her allies, they shall receive as pension, until the attainment of the age limit, the full salary last received, on the basis of which

their pension would have to be computed; they do not, however, advance according to seniority grades. After they reach the age limit, their pension is to be calculated anew according to the salary last received on the basis of which their pension was to be computed.

(3) Affairs of religious organizations are not concerned therewith.

(4) The conditions of service of teachers in public Jewish schools remain unchanged until the new regulation of the Jewish school system.

Article 5

(1) A Jew is anyone who is descended from at least three grandparents who were racially full Jews. . . .

(2) A Jew is also one who is descended from two full-Jewish grandparents if:

  (a) he belonged to the Jewish religious community at the time this law was issued or who joined the community later.

  (b) at the time the law was issued he was married to a person who was a Jew or was subsequently married to a Jew.

  (c) he is the offspring from a marriage with a Jew, in the sense of Section I, which was contracted after the coming into effect of the Law for the Protection of German Blood and Honor of September 15, 1935.

  (d) he is the offspring of an extra-marital relationship with a Jew, according to Section I, and will be born out of wedlock after July 31, 1936.

Article 6

(1) In so far as there are, in laws of the Reich or decrees of the National Socialist Labor Party and its affiliates, certain requirements for the purity of the German blood which go beyond Article 5, the same remain untouched.

(2) Other requirements for the purity of the blood that go beyond Article 5 may be submitted only with the consent of the Minister of the Interior and the Deputy to the Führer. All such requirements already in existence will be discarded after January 1, 1936 unless they have been allowed by the Minister of the Interior together with the Deputy to the Führer. Proposals for admission are to be presented to the Reich Minister of Interior.

Article 7

The Führer and Chancellor of the Reich is empowered to release anyone from the provisions of these administrative decrees.

II. THE LAW FOR THE PROTECTION OF GERMAN BLOOD AND HONOR, September 15, 1935

Imbued with the knowledge that the purity of the German blood is the necessary condition for the continued existence of the German people, and animated by the inflexible will to ensure the existence of the German nation for all future times, the Reichstag has unanimously adopted the following law which is hereby promulgated:

Article 1

(1) Marriages between Jews and subjects of German or kindred blood are forbidden. Marriages concluded despite this law are invalid, even if they are concluded abroad in order to circumvent this law.

(2) Proceedings for annulment may be initiated only by the Public Prosecutor.

Article 2

Extra-marital relations between Jews and subjects of German or kindred blood are forbidden.

Article 3

Jews may not employ in domestic service female subjects of German or kindred blood who are under the age of 45 years.

Article 4

(1) Jews are forbidden to display the Reich and national flag or to show the national colors.

(2) The display of the Jewish colors, however, is permitted for them. The exercise of this right is protected by the state.

Article 5

(1) Whoever acts in violation of the prohibition of Article 1 will be punished with penal servitude.

(2) The man who acts in violation of Article 2 will be punished with either imprisonment or penal servitude.

(3) Whoever acts in violation of Articles 3 or 4 will be punished with imprisonment up to one year and with a fine or with either of these penalties.

Article 6

The Reich Minister of Interior in conjunction with the Deputy to the Fuhrer and the Reich Minister of Justice, will issue the necessary legal and administrative decrees for the   carrying out and amplification of this law.

Article 7

This law goes into effect on the day following promulgation except for Article 3 which shall go into force on January 1, 1936.

MUNICH AGREEMENT, September 29, 1938

Adolph Hitler made great demands on Czechoslovakia, encourag-·
ing the Sudeten Nazis to force the issue. The British Prime
Minister, Neville Chamberlain, made several trips to Germany
offering concessions to Hitler, who became more demanding at
their second meeting in Godesburg. Europe was on the verge of
war when Chamberlain and Premier Edouard Daladier of France
appealed to Benito Mussolini to convince Hitler to come to some
sort of agreement. Mussolini arranged the Munich Conference
on September 28-29, 1938, which was concluded with an agreement giving Hitler the Sudeten portion of the Czechoslovak state
and leaving the latter virtually defenseless. Hitler became convinced that he could in fact gain any concession from the British
and the French.

Source: Documents and Materials Relating to the Eve of the Second World
War (New York: International Publishers, 1948), vol. I, pp. 244-251.

Germany, the United Kingdom, France and Italy, taking into consideration the agreement which has been already reached in principle
for the cession to Germany of the Sudeten German territory, have
agreed on the following terms and conditions governing the said cession
and the measures consequent thereon, and by this agreement they each
hold themselves responsible for the steps necessary to secure its ful-
fillment --
    1. The evacuation will begin on the 1st October.
    2. The United Kingdom, France and Italy agree that the evacuation
of the territory shall be completed by the 10th October, without any existing installations having been destroyed and that the Czechoslovak
Government will be held responsible for carrying out the evacuation
without damage to the said installations.
    3. The conditions governing the evacuation will be laid down in de-
tail by an international commission composed of representatives of Germany, the United Kingdom, France, Italy and Czechoslovakia.
    4. The occupation by stages of the predominantly German territory
by German troops will begin on the 1st October. . . .
    5. The international commission referred to in paragraph 3 will
determine the territories in which a plebiscite is to be held. These
territories will be occupied by international bodies until the plebiscite
has been completed. The same commission will fix the conditions in

which the plebiscite is to be held, taking as a basis the conditions of
the Saar plebiscite. The commission will also fix a date, not later than
the end of November, on which the plebiscite will be held.

6. The final determination of the frontiers will be carried out by
the international commission. This commission will also be entitled to
recommend to the four Powers - Germany, the United Kingdom, France
and Italy - in certain exceptional cases minor modifications in the
strictly ethnographical determination of the zones which are to be transferred without plebiscite.

7. There will be a right of option into and out of the transferred
territories, the option to be exercised within six months from the date
of this agreement. A German-Czechoslovak commission shall determine the details of the option, consider ways of facilitating the transfer
of population and settle questions of principle arising out of the said
transfer.

8. The Czechoslovak Government will, within a period of four weeks
from the date of this agreement, release from their military and police
forces any Sudeten Germans who may wish to be released, and the
Czechoslovak Government will within the same period, release Sudeten
German prisoners who are serving terms of imprisonment for political
offences.

Adolf Hitler
Edouard Daladier
Benito Mussolini
Neville Chamberlain

Munich, September 29, 1938

NAZI-SOVIET NON-AGGRESSION PACT

August 23, 1939

Hitler was determined to arrange an agreement with Russia before he embarked on his plan to take over Poland. He was aware
that Great Britain and France would certainly go to war, and he
wanted to avoid a two-front war in 1939 or 1940. Stalin was also
buying time, knowing that Hitler had indicated his antipathy toward the Communist State and would certainly attack. Hitler had
nothing to lose by granting concessions to Russia in Poland which
he later planned to regain.

Source: Raymond J. Stontag and James S. Beddie, eds. Nazi-Soviet
Relations, 1939-1941. Documents from the Archives of the German
Foreign Office (Washington, D.C.: Department of State Publications
No. 3023, 1948), pp. 76-78.

August 23, 1939

Treaty of Nonaggression Between Germany and the Union of Soviet
Socialist Republics

The Government of the German Reich and the Government of the Union
of Soviet Socialist Republics desirous of strengthening the cause of peace
between Germany and the U.S.S.R., and proceeding from the fundamental
provisions of the Neutrality Agreement concluded in April 1926 between
Germany and the U.S.S.R., have reached the following agreement:

ARTICLE I

Both High Contracting Parties obligate themselves to desist from any
act of violence, any aggressive action, and any attack on each other,
either individually or jointly with other powers.

ARTICLE II

Should one of the High Contracting Parties become the object of belligerent action by a third power, the other High Contracting Party shall
in no manner lend its support to this third power.

ARTICLE III

The Governments of the two High Contracting Parties shall in the future maintain continual contact with one another for the purpose of consultation in order to exchange information on problems affecting their common interests.

ARTICLE IV

Neither of the two High Contracting Parties shall participate in any grouping of powers whatsoever that is directly or indirectly aimed at the other party.

ARTICLE V

Should disputes or conflicts arise between the High Contracting Parties over problems of one kind or another, both parties shall settle these disputes or conflicts exclusively through friendly exchange of opinion or, if necessary, through the establishment of arbitration commissions.

ARTICLE VI

The present treaty is concluded for a period of ten years, with the proviso that, in so far as one of the High Contracting Parties does not denounce it one year prior to the expiration of this period, the validity of this treaty shall automatically be extended for another five years.

ARTICLE VII

The present treaty shall be ratified within the shortest possible time. The ratifications shall be exchanged in Berlin. The agreement shall enter into force as soon as it is signed.

Done in duplicate, in the German and Russian languages.

MOSCOW, August 23, 1939.

For the Government
of the German Reich:
v. RIBBENTROP

With full power of the
Government of the U.S.S.R.:
V. MOLOTOV

Secret Additional Protocol

On the occasion of the signature of the Nonaggression Pact between the German Reich and the Union of Soviet Socialist Republics the under-signed plenipotentiaries of each of the two parties discussed in strictly confidential conversations the question of the boundary of their respective spheres of influence in Eastern Europe. These conversations led to the following conclusions:

1. In the event of a territorial and political rearrangement in the areas belonging to the Baltic States (Finland, Estonia, Latvia, Lithuania) the northern boundary of Lithuania shall represent the boundary of the spheres of influence of Germany and the U.S.S.R. In this connection, the interest of Lithuania in the Vilna area is recognized by each party.

2. In the event of a territorial and political rearrangement of the areas belonging to the Polish state the spheres of influence of Germany and the U.S.S.R. shall be bounded approximately by the line of the rivers Narew, Vistula and San.

The question of whether the interests of both parties make desirable the maintenance of an independent Polish state and how such a state should be bounded can only be definitely determined in the course of fur-ther political developments.

In any event, both Governments will resolve this question by means of a friendly agreement.

3. With regard to Southeastern Europe, attention is called by the Soviet side to its interest in Bessarabia. The German side declares its complete political disinterestedness in these areas.

4. This protocol shall be treated by both parties as strictly secret.

MOSCOW, August 23, 1939.

For the Government	Plenipotentiary of the
of the German Reich:	Government of the U.S.S.R.:
v. RIBBENTROP	V. MOLOTOV

ROME-BERLIN-TOKYO AXIS, September 27, 1940

This agreement signed on September 27, 1940, was intended to pool the economic resources of the three Powers for ten years. They each recognized the others' sphere of influence and promised to cooperate in the event of war with the United States. The Treaty was not to affect the existing relationship of each with Russia. This arrangement in essence expanded the Rome-Berlin Axis into the Pact of Steel.

Source: World Almanac (New York, 1942), p. 273. - Official English translation.

The Governments of Germany, Italy and Japan, considering it as a condition precedent of any lasting peace that all nations of the world be given each its own proper place, have decided to stand by and cooperate with one another in regard to their efforts in Greater East Asia and regions of Europe respectively, wherein it is their prime purpose to establish and maintain a new order of things calculated to promote the new prosperity and welfare of the peoples concerned.

Furthermore, it is the desire of the three governments to extend cooperation to such nations in other spheres of the world as it may be inclined to put forth endeavors along lines similar to their own, in order that their ultimate aspirations for world peace may thus be realized.

Accordingly, the governments of Germany, Italy and Japan have agreed as follows:

Article 1. Japan recognizes and respects the leadership of Germany and Italy in establishment of a new order in Europe.

Article 2. Germany and Italy recognize and respect the leadership of Japan in the establishment of a new order in Greater East Asia.

Article 3. Germany, Italy and Japan agree to cooperate in their efforts on aforesaid lines. They further undertake to assist one another with all political, economic and military means when one of the three contracting powers is attacked by a power at present not involved in the European war or in the Chinese-Japanese conflict.

Article 4. With a view to implementing the present pact, joint technical commissions, members of which are to be appointed by the respective governments of Germany, Italy and Japan, will meet without delay.

Article 5. Germany, Italy and Japan affirm that the aforesaid terms do not in any way affect the political status which exists at present between each of the three contracting parties and Soviet Russia.

Article 6. The present pact shall come into effect immediately upon signature and shall remain in force ten years from the date of its coming into force. At the proper time, before the expiration of said term, the high contracting parties shall at the request of any of them, enter into negotiations for its renewal.

In faith whereof, the undersigned, duly authorized by their respective governments, have signed this pact and have affixed hereto their signatures.

Done in triplicate at Berlin, the 27th day of September 1940, in the eighteenth year of the Fascist era, corresponding to the 27th day of the ninth month of the fifteenth year of Showa (the reign of Emperor Hirohito).

YALTA CONFERENCE, February 12, 1945

President Franklin D. Roosevelt, British Prime Minister Winston Churchill, and Marshal Josef Stalin of Russia met in the Crimea in Russia during early February, 1945. At this conference, they determined their plans for the defeat, occupation and control of Germany. In addition, they made final arrangments for the United Nations Conference in San Francisco on April 25, 1945. Specific regulations were laid down in regard to Poland and Yugo-slavia.

Source: U.S. Department of State, Bulletin XII, No. 295 (February 18, 1945), pp. 213-216.

For the past eight days, Winston S. Churchill, Prime Minister of Great Britain, Franklin D. Roosevelt, President of the United States of America, and Marshal J. V. Stalin, Chairman of the Council of People's Commissars of the Union of Soviet Socialist Republics, have met with the Foreign Secretaries, Chiefs of Staff, and other Advisors in the Crimea.

The following statement is made by the Prime Minister of Great Britain, the President of the United States of America, and the Chairman of the Council of People's Commissars of the Union of Soviet Socialist Republics on the results of the Crimean Conference:

THE DEFEAT OF GERMANY

We have considered and determined the military plans of the three allied powers for the final defeat of the common enemy. The military staffs of the three allied nations have met in daily meetings throughout the Conference. These meetings have been most satisfactory from every point of view and have resulted in closer coordination of the military ef-fort of the three allies than ever before. The fullest information has been interchanged. The timing, scope and coordination of new and even more powerful blows to be launched by our armies and air forces into the heart of Germany from the East, West, North and South have been fully agreed and planned in detail.

Our combined military plans will be made known only as we execute them, but we believe that the very close working partnership among the three staffs attained at this Conference will result in shortening the War. Meetings of the three staffs will be continued in the future whenever the need arises.

Nazi Germany is doomed. The German people will only make the cost of their defeat heavier to themselves by attempting to continue a hopeless resistance.

THE OCCUPATION AND CONTROL OF GERMANY

We have agreed on common policies and plans for enforcing the unconditional surrender terms which we shall impose together on Nazi Germany after German armed resistance has been finally crushed. . . . Under the agreed plan, the forces of the three powers will each occupy a separate zone of Germany. Coordinated administration and control has been provided for under the plan through a central control commission consisting of the Supreme Commanders of the three powers with headquarters in Berlin. It has been agreed that France should be invited by the three powers . . . to participate as a fourth member of the control commission. . . .

It is our inflexible purpose to destroy German militarism and Nazism and to ensure that Germany will never again be able to disturb the peace of the world. We are determined to disarm and disband all German armed forces; . . . wipe out the Nazi Party, Nazi laws, organizations and institutions, remove all Nazi and militarist influences from public office and from the cultural and economic life of the German people. . . . It is not our purpose to destroy the people of Germany, but only when Nazism and militarism have been extirpated will there be hope for a decent life for Germans, and a place for them in the comity of nations.

REPARATION BY GERMANY

We have considered the question of the damage caused by Germany to the allied nations in this war and recognized it as just that Germany be obliged to make compensation for this damage in kind to the greatest extent possible. A commission for the compensation of damage will be established. . . .

UNITY FOR PEACE AS FOR WAR

Our meeting here in the Crimea has reaffirmed our common determination to maintain and strengthen in the peace to come that unity of purpose and of action which has made victory possible and certain for the United Nations in this war. We believe that this is a sacred obligation which our Governments owe to our peoples and to all the peoples of the world . . . . .

Victory in this war and establishment of the proposed international organization will provide the greatest opportunity in all history to create in the years to come the essential conditions of such a peace.

Signed: WINSTON S. CHURCHILL
          FRANKLIN D. ROOSEVELT
          J. STALIN

February 11, 1945.

HITLER'S POLITICAL TESTAMENT AND WILL

April 29, 1945

Hitler defended his actions since taking office. He indicated his
determination to remain in Berlin and take his life rather than be
captured. He appointed Admiral Doenitz as leader of the new
government. He praised his loyal followers. Joseph Goebbels
added that he would not honor the Fuhrer's request and would
take his own life, as well as that of his wife and children, so
that they might not suffer in the future. In Hitler's will he left
his property to the Party, or if it no longer existed, to the State.
His paintings were to go to the town of Linz.

Source: New York Times, December 30, 1945, p. 6

HITLER'S POLITICAL TESTAMENT

More than thirty years have passed since I made my modest contribution as a volunteer in the First World War, which was forced upon the
Reich.

In these last decades, love and loyalty to my people alone have
guided me in all my thoughts, actions and life. They gave me power to
make the most difficult decisions which have ever confronted mortal
man. I have spent all my time, my powers and my health in these three
decades.

It is untrue that I or anybody else in Germany wanted war in 1939.
It was wanted and provoked exclusively by those international statesmen
who either were of Jewish origin or worked for Jewish interests.

I have made too many offers of limitation and control of armaments
that posterily will not for all time be able to disregard for responsibility for the outbreak of this war to be placed on me. Furthermore, I
have never wished that after the appalling First World War there should
be a second one against either England or America. Centuries will go
by, but from the ruins of our towns and monuments the hatred of those
intimately responsible will always grow anew. They are the people
whom we have to thank for all this: International Jewry and its helpers.

Three days before the outbreak of the German-Polish War, I suggested to the British Ambassador in Berlin a solution of the German-

Polish questions, similar to that in the case of the Saar, under international control. This offer, too, cannot be denied. It was rejected
only because the ruling political clique in England wanted war, partly
for commercial reasons, partly because it was influenced by propaganda
put out by the international Jewry.

I also made it plain that if the people of Europe were again to be regarded merely as pawns in a game played by the international conspiracy
of money and finance, they, the Jews, the race that is the real guilty
party in this murderous struggle, would be saddled with the responsibility for it.

I left no one in doubt that this time not only would millions of children of European Aryan races starve, not only would millions of grown
men meet their death and not only would hundreds of thousands of women
and children be burned and bombed to death in cities, but this time the
real culprits would have to pay for their guilt even though by more hu-
mane means than war.

After six years of war, which, in spite of all setbacks, will one day
go down in history as the most glorious and heroic and manifestation of
the struggle for existence of a nation. I cannot forsake the city that is
the capital of this state. As our forces are too small to withstand an
enemy attack on this place any longer, and our own resistance will grad-
ually be worn down by men who are merely blind automatons, I wish to
share my fate with that which millions of others have also taken upon
themselves by staying in this town. Further, I shall not fall into the
hands of the enemy, who requires a new spectacle, presented by the
Jews, to divert their hysterical masses.

I have, therefore, decided to remain in Berlin and there to choose
death voluntarily at that moment when I believe that the position of the
Fuhrer and the Chancellery itself can no longer be maintained. I die
with a joyful heart in my knowledge of the immeasurable deeds and
achievements of our soldiers at the front, of our women at home, the
achievement of our peasants and workers and of a contribution unique in
history, of our youth that bears my name. . . .

From the sacrifice of our soldiers and from my own comradeship
with them to death itself, the seed has been sown that will grow one day
in the history of Germany to the glorious rebirth of the National Socialist movement and thereby to the establishment of a truly united nation.
. . . .

May it be in the future a point of honor with the German Army officers, as it is already in our navy, that the surrender of a district or

town is out of the question and that above everything else the commanders must set a shining example of faithful devotion to duty until death.

Before my death, I expel the former Reich Marshal Hermann Goering from the Party and withdraw from him all the rights that were conferred on him by the decrees of 19 June, 1941, and by my Reichstag speech of the first of September, 1939. In his place, I appoint Admiral Doenitz as President of the Reich and Supreme Commander of the armed forces.

Before my death, I expel the former Reichsfuhrer of the S.S. and the Minister of the Interior Heinrich Himmler from the party and from all his state offices. In his place, I appoint Gauleiter Karl Hanke as Reichsfuhrer of the S.S. and Chief of the German police and Gauleiter Paul Giesler as Minister of the Interior.

Apart together from their disloyalty to me, Goering and Himmler have brought irreparable shame on the country and the whole nation by secretly negotiating with the enemy without my knowledge and against my will, and also by illegally attempting to seize control of the state.

(Appoints members of new cabinet)

Although a number of these men (those appointed to the Cabinet) such as Martin Bormann, Goebbels, . . . as well as their wives have come to me of their own free will, wishing under no circumstances to leave the Reich capital, but instead to fall with me here, I must nevertheless ask them to obey my request and, in this case, put the interests of the nation above their own feelings. They will stand as near to me through their work and their loyalty as comrades after death, as I hope that my spirit will remain among them and always be with them. May they be severe but never unjust, may they above all never allow fear to influence their actions, and may they place the honor of the nation above everything on earth.

May they finally be conscious that our task, the establishment of a National Socialist State, represents the work of centuries to come and obliges each individual person always to serve the common interest before his own advantage. I ask all Germans, all National Socialists, men, women and all soldiers of the army, to be loyal and obedient to the new Government and its President.

Above all, I enjoin the Government of the Nation and the people to uphold the racial laws to the limit and to resist mercilessly the poisoner of all nations, international Jewry.

Berlin, 29 April, 1945, 0400 hours.

A. Hitler

Witnesses: Dr. Joseph Goebbels, Wilhelm Burgdorf, Martin Bormann, Hans Krebs.

APPENDIX BY GOEBBELS

The Fuhrer has ordered me to leave Berlin if the defenses of the Reich's capital collapses and take part as a leading member in the Government appointed by him.

For the first time in my life, I must categorically refuse. Apart from the fact that on the grounds of fellow-feeling and personal loyalty we could never bring ourselves to leave the Fuhrer alone in his hour of greatest need, I would otherwise appear for the rest of my life a dishonorable traitor and a common scoundrel and would lose my own self-respect, as well as the respect of my fellow-citizens, a respect that I should need in any further service in the future rebuilding of the German nation and the German state.

In the nightmare of treason that surrounds the Fuhrer in these most critical days of the war, there must be at least some people to stay with him unconditionally until death, even if this contradicts the formal and, from a material point of view, entirely justifiable order that he gives in his political testament.

I believe that I am thereby doing the best service to the future of the German people. In the hard times to come, examples will be more important than men. Men will always be found to show the nation the way out of its tribulations, but a reconstruction of the national life would be impossible if it were not inspired by examples that are clear and easily understandable.

For this reason, together with my wife and on behalf of my children, who are too young to be able to speak for themselves, and who if they were sufficiently old, would agree with this decision without reservation, I express my unalterable decision not be leave the Reich capital even if it falls, and at the side of the Fuhrer to end a life that for me personally will have no further value, if I cannot spend it at the service of the Fuhrer and at his side.

HITLER'S PERSONAL WILL

Although during the years of struggle, I believed that I would not undertake the responsibility of marriage, now, before the end of my life, I have decided to take as my wife, the woman, who, after many years of true friendship, came to this city almost already besieged, of her own free will in order to share my fate.

She will go to her death with me at her own wish as my wife. This will compensate us both for what we both lost through my work in the service of my people.

My possessions, in so far as they are worth anything, belong to the party, or, if this no longer exists, to the state. If the state, too, is destroyed, there is no need for any further instructions on my part. The paintings in the collections bought by me during the years were never assembled for private purposes but solely for the establishment of a picture gallery in my home town of Linz on the Danube.

It is my heartfelt wish that this will should duly be executed. As executor, I appoint my most faithful party comrade, Martin Bormann. He receives full legal authority to make all decisions. He is permitted to hand over to my relatives everything that is of value as a personal memento, or is necessary for maintaining a petit-bourgeois standard of living, especially to my wife's mother and my faithful fellow-workers of both sexes who are well-known to him.

The chief of these are my former secretaries, Frau Winter, etc., who helped me for many years by their work.

My wife and I choose to die in order to escape the shame of our wish for our bodies to be cremated immediately on the place where I have performed the greater part of my daily work during twelve years of service to my people.

Berlin, 29 April, 1400 hours.

                                        A. Hitler

Witnesses: Martin Bormann, Dr. Joseph Goebbels, Nicolaus von Buelow.

ACT OF MILITARY SURRENDER, May 7, 1945

General Gustav Jodl, representing the German High Command
and Admiral Doenitz, Hitler's successor, signed the terms of
surrender on May 7, 1945, at 2:41 A.M., at Rheims, France.
All hostilities were to end at 11:01 P.M.

Source: U.S. Department of State, Bulletin, XII, No. 317 (July 22,
1945), p. 106.

1. We the undersigned, acting by authority of the German High Command, hereby surrender unconditionally to the Supreme Commander,
Allied Expeditionary Force and simultaneously to the Soviet High Command all forces on land, sea, and in the air who are at this date under
German control.

2. The German High Command will at once issue orders to all
German military, naval and air authorities and to all forces under German control to cease active operations at 2301 hours Central European
time on 8 May and to remain in the positions occupied at that time. No
ship, vessel, or aircraft is to be scuttled, or any damage done to their
hull, machinery or equipment.

3. The German High Command will at once issue to the appropriate
commanders, and ensure the carrying out of any further orders issued
by the Supreme Commander, Allied Expeditionary Force and by the
Soviet High Command.

4. This act of military surrender is without prejudice to, and will
be superseded by any general instrument of surrender imposed by, or
on behalf of the United Nations and applicable to GERMANY and the
German armed forces as a whole.

5. In the event of the German High Command or any of the forces
under their control failing to act in accordance with this Act of Surrender, the Supreme Commander, Allied Expeditionary Force and the
Soviet High Command will take such punitive or other action as they
deem appropriate.

Signed at Rheims at 0241 on the 7th day of May, 1945
                                      France
On behalf of the German High Command.
                          JODL

                          IN THE PRESENCE OF:

On behalf of the Supreme   On behalf of the Soviet
     Commander, Allied Ex-   High Command.
     peditionary Force.   SOUSLOPAROV
          W. B. SMITH

F. SEVEZ
     Major General, French Army
               (Witness)

THE BONN CONSTITUTION, May 23, 1949

With AMENDMENTS

The German Republic came into existence in 1949. The three Western Powers permitted the establishment of a Parliamentary Council on September 1, 1948 to draw up a Constitution. This Council sat under the Presidency of Konrad Adenauer until May 23, 1949, when it adopted the "Basic Law" or German Constitution which was then approved by the U.S., Great Britain and France. The Constitution has since been revised and amended. The following extracts illustrate the basic concepts and aims of the West German State.

Source: The Bonn Constitution: Basic Law for the Federal Republic, Washington, D.C.: U.S. Government Printing Office, 1949. See also The Bonn Constitution with Amendments: Basic Law for the Federal Republic (New York, n.d.)

PREAMBLE

The German People in the Länder of Braden, Bavaria, Bremen, Hamburg, Hesse, Lower Saxony, North Rhine-Westphalia, Rhineland-Palatinate, Schleswig-Holstein, Wurttemberg-Baden, and Wurttemberg-Hohenzollern,
Conscious of its responsibility before God and Men,
Animated by the resolve to preserve its national and political unity and to serve the peace of the World as an equal partner in a united Europe,
Desiring to give a new order to political life for a transitional period, has enacted, by virtue of its constituent power, this Basic Law of the Federal Republic of Germany.
It has also acted on behalf of those Germans to whom participation was denied.
The entire German people is called on to achieve by free self-determination the unity and freedom of Germany.

I. BASIC RIGHTS

Article 1 *

1) The dignity of man is inviolable. To respect and protect it is the duty of all state authority.

2) The German people therefore acknowledge inviolable and inalienable human rights as the basis of every community, of peace and of justice in the world.

3) The following basic rights bind the legislature, the executive and the judiciary as directly enforceable law.

* As amended by Federal Law of March 19, 1956

Article 2

1) Everyone has the right to the free development of his personality insofar as he does not violate the rights of others or offend against the constitutional order or the moral code.

2) Everyone has the right to life and to inviolability of his person. The freedom of the individual is inviolable. These rights may only be encroached upon pursuant to a law.

Article 3

1) All persons are equal before the law.

2) Men and women have equal rights.

3) No one may be prejudiced or favored because of his sex, his parentage, his race, his language, his homeland and origin, his faith or his religious or political opinions.

Article 4

1) Freedom of faith and of conscience, and freedom of creed, religious or ideological, are inviolable.

2) The undisturbed practice of religion is guaranteed.

3) No one may be compelled against his conscience to render war service as an armed combatant. Details will be regulated by a Federal Law.

Article 5

1) Everyone has the right freely to express and to disseminate his opinion by speech, writing and pictures and freely to inform himself from generally accessible source. Freedom of the press and freedom of reporting by radio and motion pictures are guaranteed. There shall be no censorship.

2) These rights are limited by the provisions of the general laws, the provisions of law for the protection of youth and by the right to inviolability of personal honor.

3) Art and science, research and teaching are free. Freedom of teaching does not absolve from loyalty to the constitution.

Article 6

1) Marriage and family enjoy the special protections of the state.

2) Care and upbringing of children are the natural right of the parents and a duty primarily incumbent on them. The state watches over the performance of this duty. . . .

4) Every mother is entitled to the protection and care of the community. . . .

Article 7

1) The entire educational system is under the supervision of the state.

2) The persons entitled to bring up a child have the right to decide whether it shall receive religious instruction. . . .

Article 8

1) All Germans have the right to assemble peacefully and unarmed without prior notification or permission.

2) With regard to open-air meetings this right may be restricted by or pursuant to a law.

Article 9

1) All Germans have the right to form associations and societies. . . .

Article 10

Secrecy of the mail and secrecy of posts and telecommunications are inviolable. Restrictions may be ordered only pursuant to a law.

Article 11

1) All Germans enjoy freedom of movement throughout the Federal territory.

2) This right may be restricted only by a law and only in cases in which an adequate basis of existence is lacking and special burdens would arise to the community as a result thereof or in which the restriction is necessary for the protection of youth against neglect, for combating the danger of epidemics or for the prevention of crime.

Article 12 *

1) All Germans have the right freely to choose their trade or profession, their place of work and their place of training. The practice of trades and professions may be regulated by law. . . .

3) Women shall not be required by law to render service in any unit of the Armed Forces. On no account shall they be employed in any service involving the use of arms.

4) Forced labor may be imposed only in the event that a person is deprived of his freedom by the sentence of a court.

Article 13

1) The home is inviolable.

2) Searchers may be ordered only by a judge or, in the event of danger in delay, by other organs as provided by law, and may be carried out only in the form prescribed by law. . . .

Article 14

1) Property and the rights of inheritance are guaranteed. Their content and limits are determined by the laws.

3) Expropriation is permitted only in the public weal. It may take place only by or pursuant to a law which provides for kind and extent of the compensation. . . .

Article 15

Land, natural resources and means of production may for the purpose of socialization be transferred into public ownership or other forms of publicly controlled economy by a law which provided for kin and extent of the compensation. With respect to such compensation Article 14, paragraph 3, sentences 3 and 4, apply mutatis mutandis.

* As amended by Federal Law of March 19, 1956

II. THE FEDERATION AND THE LANDER

Article 20

1) The Federal Republic of Germany is a democratic and social federal state.

2) All state authority emanates from the people. It is exercised by the people by means of elections and voting and by separate legislative, executive, and judicial organs.

3) Legislation is subject to the constitutional order; the executive and the judiciary are bound by law.

Article 21

1) The political parties participate in the forming of the political will of the people. They may be freely formed. . . .

Article 24

1) The Federation may, by legislation, transfer sovereign powers to international institutions.

2) For the maintenance of peace, the Federation may join a system of mutual collective security; . . .

III. THE BUNDESTAG

Article 38

1) The deputies to the German Bundestag are elected in universal, direct, free, equal and secret elections. They are representatives of the whole people, are not bound by orders and instructions and are subject only to their conscience.

2) Anyone who has attained the age of twenty-five is eligible for election. . . .

Article 39

1) The Bundestag is elected for a four-year term. . . .

Article 44

1) The Bundestag has the right, and upon the motion of one-fourth of its members the duty, to set up a committee of investigation which shall take the requisite evidence at public hearings. The public may be excluded. . . .

Article 45

1) The Bundestag appoints a Standing Committee which shall safeguard the rights of the Bundestag as against the Federal Government in the interval between two legislative terms. The Standing Committee has also the powers of a committee of investigation. . . .

Article 45a*

1) The Bundestag shall appoint a Committee on Foreign Affairs and

* Amended by Federal Law of March 19, 1956

158 GERMANY

a Committee on Defense. Both committees shall function also in the intervals between any two legislative terms. . . .

IV. THE BUNDESRAT

Article 50

The Länder participate through the Bundesrat in the legislation and administration of the Federation.

Article 51

1) The Bundesrat consists of members of the Länder governments which appoint and recall them. Other members of such governments may act as substitutes.

2) Each Land has at least three votes; Länder with more than two million inhabitants have four, Länder with more than six million inhabitants, five votes. . . .

V. THE FEDERAL PRESIDENT

Article 54

1) The Federal President is elected, without debate, by the Federal Convention. Every German is eligible who is entitled to vote for the Bundestag and who has attained the age of forty.

2) The term of office of the Federal President is five years. Reelection for a consecutive term is permitted only once.

3) The Federal Convention consists of the members of the Bundestag and an equal number of members elected by the representative assemblies of the Länder according to the rules of proportional representation. . . .

Article 56

On assuming his office the Federal President takes the following oath before the assembled members of the Bundestag and the Bundesrat.

"I swear that I will dedicate my efforts to the well-being of the German people, enhance its benefits, ward harm from it, uphold and defend the Basic Law and the laws of the Federation, fulfill my duties conscientiously, and do justice to all. So help me God."

The oath may also be taken without religious affirmation.

Article 59

1) The Federal President represents the Federation in its international relations. He concludes treaties with foreign states on behalf of the Federation. He accredits and receives envoys. . . .

VI. THE FEDERAL GOVERNMENT

Article 62

The Federal Government consists of the Federal Chancellor and the Federal Ministers.

Article 63

1) The Federal Chancellor is elected, without debate, by the Bundestag

on the proposal of the Federal President. . . .

Article 65
    The Federal Chancellor determines, and is responsible for, general policy. Within the limits of this general policy, each Federal Minister conducts the business of his department autonomously and on his own responsibility. The Federal Government decides on differences of opinion between the Federal Ministers. The Federal Chancellor conducts the business of the Federal Government in accordance with rules of procedure adopted by it and approved by the Federal President.

Article 77
    1) Federal laws are adopted by the Bundestag. Upon their adoption, they shall, without delay, be transmitted to the Bundesrat by the President of the Bundestag.
    2) The Bundesrat may, within two weeks of the receipt of the adopted bill, demand that a committee for joint consideration of bills, composed of members of the Bundestag and the Bundesrat, be convened.

Article 79 *
    1) The Basic Law can be amended only by a law which expressly amends or supplements the text thereof.
    3) An amendment of this Basic Law affecting the division of the Federation into Länder, the participation in principle of the Länder in legislation, or the basic principles laid down in Articles 1 and 20, is inadmissible.

Article 80
    1) The Federal Government, a Federal Minister, or the Land Governments may be authorized by a law to issue ordinances having the force of law. The content, purpose and scope of the powers conferred must be set forth in the law. The legal basis must be stated in the ordinance. If a law provides that a power may be further delegated, an ordinance having the force of law is necessary in order to delegate the power.
    2) The consent of the Bundesrat is required, unless otherwise provided by Federal legislation, for ordinances having the force of law issued by the Federal Government or a Federal Minister concerning basic rules for the use of facilities of the Federal railroads and of postal and telecommunication services, or charges therefore, or concerning the construction and operation of railroads, as well as for ordinances having the force of law issued on the basis of Federal laws that require the consent of the Bundesrat or that are executed by the Länder as agents of the Federation or as matters of their own concern.

IX. THE ADMINISTRATION OF JUSTICE

Article 92
    The judicial authority is vested in the judges; it is exercised by the Federal Constitutional Court, by the Supreme Federal Court, by the Federal courts provided for in this Basic Law and by the courts of the Länder. . . .

* As amended by Federal Law of December 23, 1956

Article 97

1) The judges are independent and subject only to the law.

2) Judges appointed permanently on a full time basis to an established post can, against their will, be dismissed, or permanently or temporarily suspended from office, or transferred to another post, or retired before expiration of their term of office only under authority of a judicial decision and only on grounds and in the form provided for by law. Legislation may set age limits for the retirement of judges appointed for life.

Article 104

1) The freedom of the individual may be restricted only on the basis of a formal law and only with due regard to the forms prescribed therein. Detained persons may be subjected neither to mental nor to physical ill-treatment.

2) Only judges may decide on admissibility or extension of a deprivation of liberty.

3) Any person provisionally detained on suspicion of having committed a punishable offense must be brought before a judge at the latest on the day following the arrest; . . .

4) A relative of the person detained or a person enjoying his confidence must be notified without delay of any judicial decision ordering or extending a deprivation of liberty.

<h3 style="text-align:center">X. FINANCE</h3>

Article 105

1) The Federation has the exclusive power to legislate on customs and fiscal monopolies. . . .

<h3 style="text-align:center">XI. TRANSITIONAL AND CONCLUDING PROVISIONS</h3>

Article 116

1) Unless otherwise provided by law, a German within the meaning of this Basic Law is a person who possesses German citizenship or who has been admitted to the territory of the German Reich, as it existed on December 31, 1937, as a refugee or expellee of German stock or as the spouse or descendant of such person.

2) Former German citizens who, between January 30, 1933 and May 8, 1945, were deprived of their citizenship for political, racial or religious reasons, and their descendants, shall be re-granted German citizenship on application.

Article 140

The provisions of Articles 136, 137, 138, 139 and 141 of the German Constitution of August 11, 1919, are an integral part of this Basic Law. . . .

Article 146

This Basic Law shall cease to be in force on the day on which a constitution adopted by a free decision of the German people comes into force.

Bonn/Rhine, May 23, 1949.

APPENDIX TO BASIC LAW

Articles 136-137-138-139 and 141 of the Section "RELIGION AND RELIGIOUS ASSOCIATIONS" of the Weimar Constitution incorporated into the Basic law for the Federal Republic of Germany pursuant to Article 140 thereof.

Article 136

Civil and political rights and duties are neither dependent upon nor restricted by the practice of religious freedom.

The enjoyment of civil and political rights, as well as admission to official posts, is independent of religious creed.

No one is bound to disclose his religious convictions. The authorities have the right to make enquiries as to membership of a religious body only when rights and duties depend upon it, or when the collection of statistics ordered by law requires it. No one may be compelled to take part in any ecclesiatical act or ceremony, or the use of any religious form of oath.

Article 137

There is no state church.

Freedom of association is guaranteed to religious bodies. There are no restrictions as to the union of religious bodies within the territory of the Federation.

Each religious body regulates and administers its affairs independently within the limits of general laws. It appoints its officials without the co-operation of the Land, or of the civil community.

Religious bodies acquire legal rights in accordance with the general regulations of the civil code.

Religious bodies remain corporations with public rights in so far as they have been so up to the present.

Equal rights shall be granted to other religious bodies upon application, if their constitution and the number of their members offer a guarantee of permanency.

When several such religious bodies holding public rights combine to form one union this union becomes a corporation of similar class.

Religious bodies forming corporations with public rights are entitled to levy taxes on the basis of the civil tax-rolls, in accordance with the provisions of Land law.

Associations adopting as their work the common encouragement of a world-philosophy shall be placed upon an equal footing with religious bodies.

So far as the execution of these provisions may require further regulation, this is the duty of the Land legislature.

Article 138

Land connections with religious bodies, depending upon law, agreement or special legal titles, are dissolved by Land legislation. The principle for such action shall be laid down by the Federal Government.

Ownership and other rights of religious bodies and unions to their institutions, foundations and other properties devoted to purposes of public worship, education or charity, are guaranteed.

Article 139

Sundays and holidays recognized by the <u>Land</u> shall remain under legal protection as days of rest from work and for the promotion of spiritual purpose.

Article 141

Religious bodies shall have the right of entry for religious purposes into the army, hospitals, prisons, or other public institutions, so far as is necessary for the arrangement of public worship or the exercise of pastoral offices, but every form of compulsion must be avoided.

BERLIN DECLARATION ON GERMAN REUNIFICATION

ISSUED BY FOUR WESTERN POWERS, July 29, 1957

Britain, France, the United States, and West Germany indicated their continued desire to see Germany reunified. They also claimed that a reunited Germany should be free to determine the direction of its political development as well as its diplomatic arrangements.

Source: U.S. Department of State, Bulletin, XXXVII, No. 947 (August 19, 1957), pp. 304-306.

Twelve years have elapsed since the end of the war in Europe. The hopes of the peoples of the world for the establishment of a basis for a just and lasting peace have nevertheless not been fulfilled. One of the basic reasons for the failure to reach a settlement is the continued division of Germany, which is a grave injustice to the German people and the major source of international tension in Europe.

The Governments of France, the United Kingdom and the United States, which share with the Soviet Union responsibility for the reunification of Germany and the conclusion of a peace treaty, and the Government of the Federal Republic of Germany, as the only Government qualified to speak for the German people as a whole, wish to declare their views on these questions, including the question of European security, and the principles which motivate their policies in this regard.

1. A European settlement must be based on freedom and justice. Every nation has the right to determine its own way of life in freedom, to determine for itself its political, economic and social system, and to provide for its security with due regard to the legitimate interests of other nations. . . .

2. The reunification of Germany remains the joint responsibility of the Four Powers who in 1945 assumed supreme authority in Germany. . . . At the same time the achievement of German reunification requires the active cooperation of the German people as a whole under conditions ensuring the free expression of their will.

3. The unnatural division of Germany and of its capital, Berlin, is a continuing source of international tension. So long as Germany remains divided there can be no German peace treaty and no assurance of stability in Europe. The reunification of Germany in freedom is not only an elementary requirement of justice for the German people, but is the only sound basis of a lasting settlement in Europe.

4. Only a freely elected all-German Government can undertake on behalf of a reunified Germany obligations which will inspire confidence on the part of other countries and which will be considered just and binding in the future by the people of Germany themselves.

5. Such a Government can only be established through free elections throughout Germany for an all-German National Assembly.

6. There should be no discrimination against a reunified Germany. Its freedom and security should not be prejudiced by an imposed status of neutralization or demilitarization. Its Government should be free to determine its foreign policy and to decide on its international associations. It should not be deprived of the right recognized in the Charter of the United Nations for all nations to participate in collective measures of self-defense.

7. Re-establishment of the national unity of Germany in accordance with the freely expressed wishes of the German people would not in itself constitute a threat to Germany's neighbors nor would it prejudice their security. Nevertheless, so as to meet any preoccupation which other governments may have in this respect, appropriate arrangements, linked with German reunification, should be made which would take into account the legitimate security interests of all the countries concerned. . . .

8. The Western Powers have never required as a condition of German reunification that a reunified Germany should join the North Atlantic Treaty Organization. It will be for the people of a reunified Germany themselves to determine through their freely elected Government whether they wish to share in the benefits and obligations of the treaty.

9. If the all-German Government, in the exercise of its free choice, should elect to join NATO, the Western Powers after consultation with other members of NATO are prepared to offer on a basis of reciprocity, to the Government of the Soviet Union and the Governments of other countries of Eastern Europe which would become parties to a European security arrangement, assurances of a significant and far-reaching character. . . .

11. The reunification of Germany accompanied by the conclusion of European security arrangements would facilitate the achievement of a comprehensive disarmament agreement. Conversely, if a beginning could be made toward effective measures of partial disarmament, this would contribute to the settlement of outstanding major political problems. . . . The Western Powers do not intend to enter into any agreement on disarmament which would prejudice the reunification of Germany.

12. Any measures of disarmament applicable to Europe must have the consent of the European nations concerned and take into account the link between European security and German reunification. The Four Governments continue to hope that the Soviet Government will come to recognize that it is not in its own interest to maintain the present division of Germany. . . .

BIBLIOGRAPHY

The works cited in the bibliography are critically selected to cover the broad spectrum of German History. Those chosen are all written or translated into English for the benefit of undergraduate research. Many of the monographs have more detailed bibliographies of their periods with works both in English and German. Students might also wish to consult Historical Abstracts, Reader's Guide to Periodical Literature, and Social Sciences and Humanities Index for recent articles in scholarly journals.

Asterisks after titles indicate those books available in paperback editions.

SOURCES

Böhme, Helmut, ed. The Foundation of the German Empire: Selected Documents. Agatha Ramm, trans. London, 1971.

Dugdale, E. T. S., ed. and trans. German Diplomatic Documents, 1871-1914. 2 vols. New York, 1929.

German Library of Information. Documents on the Events Preceding the Outbreak of the War. New York, 1940.

Hertslet, Edward, ed. The Map of Europe by Treaty. 3 vols. London, 1875. Good for all basic treaties and conventions.

Lord, Robert H. The Origins of the War of 1870. New Documents from the German Archives. New York, 1966. Good analysis of the period preceding the war. Documents mainly in German.

Lutz, Ralph H., lit. ed. Fall of the German Empire. Hoover War Library Publications Nos. 1 and 2. Stanford Univ., California, 1932.

Snyder, Louis L., ed. Documents of German History. New Brunswick, New Jersey, 1958. Covers entire period.

Montegelas, Max and Schucking, Walther, eds. Outbreak of the World War. German Documents Collected by Karl Kautsky. Trans. by Carnegie Endowment for International Peace. Division of International Law, New York, 1924.

Sontag, Raymond J. and Beddie, James S., eds. Nazi-Soviet Relations, 1939-1941. Documents from the Archives of the German Foreign Office. Department of State Publications, No. 3023. Washington, D. C., 1948.

U. S. Congress. Senate. Committee on Foreign Relations. Documents on Germany, 1944-1961. Washington D. C., 1961

GENERAL HISTORIES

Atkinson, Christopher. A History of Germany, 1715-1815. Westport, Conn., 1971. Well-detailed analysis of the period.

Barraclough, Geoffrey. The Origins of Modern Germany. Oxford, 1962. Fine Study of early years of German development.

Carr, William. A History of Germany, 1815-1945. New York, 1969. Straightforward account for undergraduate and other readers.

Dehio, Ludwig. Germany and World Politics in the Twentieth Century. New York, 1960. Study of various aspects of German and world diplomacy.

Dill, Marshall. Germany, A Modern History. Ann Arbor, Mich., 1961. Well-balanced, readable concise account.

Flenley, Ralph. Modern German History. New York, 1964. Good discussion of German History.

Gooch, George P. Studies in German History. New York, 1969. 2nd ed. Many items illustrating almost every phase of German history from the Reformation to outbreak of World War II.

Holborn, Hajo. A History of Modern Germany. 3 vols. New York, 1959. Fine comprehensive study from Reformation to 1945.

Mann, Golo. The History of Germany Since 1789. New York, 1968. Fine account of past two centuries.

Pinson, Koppel S. Modern Germany, Its History and Civilization. New York, 1954. Many quotations in this thoughtful work.

Reinhardt, Kurt F. Germany: 2000 Years. New York, 1950. Fine account emphasizing cultural aspects with many dates and facts.

Vermeil, Edmond. Germany's Three Reichs; Their History and Culture. trans. E. W. Dickes. New York, 1969. Good interpretative treatment of German culture.

PRUSSIA, AUSTRIA, AND THE GERMANIC EMPIRE

Carsten, Francis L. The Origins of Prussia. Oxford, 1954. First thoroughgoing account in English.

Ergang, Robert. The Potsdam Fuhrer. New York, 1941. First biography in English.

Fay, Sidney B. The Rise of Brandenburg-Prussia to 1786. New York, 1964. Best short account of early Prussia.

Gaxotte, Pierre. Frederick the Great. New Haven, Conn., 1942. Fine concise account.

Gooch, George P. Frederick the Great, the Ruler, the Writer, the Man. New York, 1947. Fair, moderate account.

Langsam, Walter C. Francis the Good: The Education of an Emperor, 1768-1792. New York, 1949. Based on scholarly sources.

Padover, Saul K. The Revolutionary Emperor: Joseph the Second. 2nd rev. ed. Hamden, Conn., 1967. Sympathetic account.

Reddaway, William F. Frederick the Great and the Rise of Prussia. New York, 1969. Fine account of this important 18th century ruler.

Schevill, Ferdinand. The Great Elector. Hamden, Conn., 1965. Fine analysis of Frederick William.

Wedgwood, Cicely Veronica. The Thirty Years War. London, 1944. Well-written detailed analysis of the war.

THE GERMANIC CONFEDERATION

Eyck, Frank. The Frankfurt Parliament, 1848-1849. New York, 1968. Detailed analysis of workings and results of the assembly.

Ford, Guy S. Stein and the Era of Reform in Prussia, 1807-1815. Princeton, 1922. Valuable account of the man and his work.

Gooch, George P. Germany and the French Revolution. New York, 1920. Good account about important period in German affairs.

Hamerow, T. S. Restoration, Revolution, Reaction; Economics and Politics in Germany, 1815-1871. Princeton, 1958. New information on economic and social aspects of years before 1848 and the Revolutions.

Henderson, William O. The Zollverein. Cambridge, Eng., 1939. Standard work, detailed especially in diplomatic field.

Namier, Lewis B. 1848: The Revolution of the Intellectuals. London, 1944. Good analysis of liberals' attempts to take control and why they failed.

Noyes, P. H. Organization and Revolution: Working-Class Associations in the German Revolutions of 1848-1849. Princeton, 1966. Traces various associations behind revolution.

Robertson, Priscilla. Revolutions of 1848, A Social History. New York, 1960. Well-written analysis with many facts.*

Sontag, Raymond. Germany and England. Background for Conflict, 1848-1918. Intensive study which tries to discover why these two "natural allies" became "natural enemies."

Valentin, Veit. 1848; Chapters of German History. Trans. Ethel Talbot. London, 1940. Picture of various aspects of Germany.

Whitridge, Arnold. Men in Crisis: The Revolutions of 1848. Hamden, Conn, 1967. Discussion of various individuals who led or opposed the Revolution.

BISMARCK AND THE GERMAN EMPIRE

Bismarck, Otto fürst von. Bismarck, the Man and the Statesman; Being the Reflections and Reminiscences of Otto, Prince von Bismarck, Written and Dictated by Himself After His Retirement from Office. trans. A. J. Butler. New York, 1968.*

Brandenburg, Erich. From Bismarck to the World War: A History of German Foreign Policy, 1870-1914. Trans. Anne E. Adams. London, 1927. Strongly pro-German but does criticize short-sightedness of German policy.

Busch, Moritz. Our Chancellor (Bismarck); Sketches for a Historical Picture. Trans. William Beatty-Kingston. Freeport, N. Y. 1970. Good general description.

Carroll, Eber M. Germany and the Foreign Powers, 1866-1914. A Study in Public Opinion and Foreign Policy. New York, 1938. Shows public views as indicated in newspapers.

Darmstaedter, Friedrich. Bismarck and the Creation of the Second Reich. London, 1948. Fine analysis of unification movement.

Eyck, Erich. Bismarck and the German Empire. London, 1950. Political biography presenting statecraft of Bismarck.

Hamerow, Theodore S. The Social Foundations of German Unification, 1858-1871. Princeton, 1969. Good discussion of social issues.

Joll, James. The Second International, 1889-1914. New York, 1966. International description of Social Democratic Party.

Lord, Robert H. Origins of the War of 1870; New Documents from the German Archives. New York, 1966. Pro-French. Good analysis, as well as source of documents mainly in German.

Simon, Walter M. Germany in the Age of Bismarck. New York, 1968. Comprehensive study of era. Good documents.

Pflanze, Otto. Bismarck and the Development of Germany. The Period of Unification, 1815-1871. Princeton, 1963. 1st volume blames Bismarck for widening gap between Western ideas and German political attitudes.

Sontag, Raymond. European Diplomatic History, 1871-1932. New York, 1961. Brief sketch of diplomatic relations among great European powers.

Steefel, Lawrence D. The Schleswig-Holstein Question. Cambridge, Mass., 1932. Fine study of complicated problems involved with duchies.

Sybel, Heinrich von. The Founding of the German Empire by William I. Trans. Marshall Livingston Perrin and Gamaliel Bradford, Jr., 7 vols. New York, 1968. Detailed analysis of unification period.

Taylor, Alan J. P. Bismarck, the Man and the Statesman. New York, York, 1955. Brief over-all biography.

THE ERA OF WILLIAM II

Albertini, Luigi. Origins of the War of 1914. Trans. Isabella M. Massey. 3 vols. New York, 1952-1957. Well-written with much detail.

Aronson, Theo. The Kaisers. Indianapolis, 1971. Centering on Hohenzollerns of 2nd Empire.

Barnes, Harry E. The Genesis of the World War. New York, 1970. Good discussion of revisionist views, questions blame of Germany.

Fay, Sidney B. Origins of the World War. New York, 1928. Revisionist questioning myth of Germany's sole responsibility for the war.

Gauss, Christian. The German Emperor as Shown in His Public Utterances. New York, 1915. Good collection of speeches.

Kurenberg, Joachim von. The Kaiser; A Life of Wilhelm II, Last Emperor of Germany. Trans. H. T. Russell and Herta Hagen. New York, 1955. Biography written by German nobleman.

Langer, William L. European Alliances and Alignments, 1871-1890. New York, 1964. Uses new material to study Bismarckian era.

---------------- The Diplomacy of Imperialism, 1890-1902. New York, 1935. Carries previous work further, considers every important problem in European diplomatic history.

Ludwig, Emil. Wilhelm Hohenzollern, the Last of the Kaisers. trans. Ethel C. Mayne, New York, 1927. Important study of his activities and actions.

Massing, Paul W. Rehearsal for Destruction: A Study of Political Anti-Semitism in Imperial Germany. New York, 1949. Shows use of anti-semitism as tool by those who understood its potential.

Nichols, John A. Germany After Bismarck, the Caprivi Era, 1890-1894. Cambridge, Mass., 1958. First full-scale treatment of Bismarck's successor, discussing machinery of government.

Nowak, Karl F. Kaiser and Chancellor; the Opening Years of the Reign of Kaiser Wilhelm II. trans. E. W. Dickes. New York, 1930. Explains breach with Bismarck using official documents.

------------------ Germany's Road to Ruin; the Middle Years of the Reign of Emperor Wilhelm II. trans. E. W. Dickes. New York, 1932. Personal and psychological aspects.

Rohl, John C. G. Germany without Bismarck; the Crisis of Government in the Second Reich, 1890-1900. Berkeley, Calif., 1967. Illustrates intrigues in high levels of German government.

Rosenberg, Arthur. The Birth of the German Republic, 1871-1918. Trans. Ian F. D. Morrow. New York, 1964. Good background for birth of Weimar Republic and failure in war.*

Schmitt, Bernadotte E. The Coming of the War, 1914. 2 vols. New York 1930. Study of immediate origins of war.

Wertheimer, Mildred S. The Pan-German League, 1890-1914. New York, 1924. Important study of this nationalist organization.

THE WEIMAR REPUBLIC

Berlau, A. Joseph. The German Social Democratic Party, 1914-1921. New York, 1970. Study of problems and final defeat of the Social Democratic Organization. Indicates conditions preceding rise of Nazis.

Brecht, Arnold. Prelude to Silence, The End of the German Republic. New York, 1968. Good analysis of reasons for end of Republic and triumph of Nazis.

Clark, Robert T. The Fall of the German Republic, A Political Study. New York, 1964. Fine study of political reasons for failure of Republic.

Coper, Rudolf. Failure of a Revolution; Germany in 1918-1919. Cambridge, Eng., 1955. Important study of Socialist uprising.

Eyck, Erich. A History of the Weimar Republic. Trans. Harlan P. Hanson and Robert G. L. Waite. 2 vols. Cambridge, Mass., 1962. Good detailed study of Weimar.

Fraser, Lindley M. Germany Between Two Wars, A Study of Propaganda and War Guilt. New York, 1945. Indicates myth by which German propagandists explained away defeat in First World War and disguised causes of Second.

Halperin, Samuel W. Germany Tried Democracy, A Political History of the Reich from 1918 to 1933. Hampden, Conn. 1963. Good analysis of Weimar and reasons for triumph of the Nazis.*

Hunt, Richard N., ed. The Creation of the Weimar Republic; Stillborn Democracy? Lexington, Mass., 1969. Series of selections describing problems and why it failed.*

McKenzie, John Richard P. Weimar Germany, 1918-1933. Totowa, N.J., 1971. Political study of period.

Olden, Rudolf. Stresemann. Trans. R. T. Clark. New York, 1930. Biography as well as review of German politics in Weimar period.

Waldman, Eric. The Spartacist Uprising of 1919 and the Crisis of the German Socialist Movement: A Study of the Relation of Political Theory and Party Practice. Milwaukee, Wisc., 1958. Important study of the Socialist movement and failure.

Watt, Richard M. The Kings Depart; The Tragedy of Germany: Versailles and the German Revolution. New York, 1969. Good biographical sketches of all major figures.

Wheeler-Bennett, Sir John. Hindenburg: The Wooden Titan. New York, 1967. Good study of his role as military and political figure.

THE THIRD REICH: NAZI DICTATORSHIP

Allen, William S. The Nazi Seizure of Power: The Experience of a Single German Town, 1930-1935. Chicago, 1965. Factual report of how Nazis took over small German town, indicating how terror succeeded.*

Boehm, Erich H. We Survived; Fourteen Histories of the Hidden and Hunted of Nazi Germany. Santa Barbara, Calif., 1966. Good background of the terror tactics.*

Bullock, Alan. Hitler, A Study in Tyranny. New York, 1952. Complete biography of the character, career and evil influence which Hitler exerted on modern times.*

Butler, Rohan d'O. The Roots of National Socialism, 1783-1933. New York, 1968. Critical study of origins of National Socialism.

Davidson, Eugene. The Death and Life of Germany. New York, 1959.
    Chronological study of major events showing views of policy makers
    and ordinary people.

Dulles, Allen W. Germany's Underground. New York, 1947. Indicates
    part played by generals, politicians, and others which ended in at-
    tempted assassination of Hitler in July, 1944.

Gilbert, Felix. Hitler Directs His War; The Secret Records of His
    Daily Military Conferences. New York, 1950. Shows complex as-
    pects of Hitler's character.

Hansen, Richard. Putsch! How Hitler Made Revolution. New York,
    1970. Discusses his early life and details of Munich Putsch.

Herzstein, Robert E., comp. Adolph Hitler and the Third Reich, 1933-
    1945. Boston, 1971. Essays on various aspects of life in Germany.
Hitler, Adolph. Mein Kampf. Trans. Ralph Mannteim. Boston, 1943.*
Jarman, Thomas L. The Rise and Fall of Nazi Germany. New York,
    1956. Good general study of the period.*

Lichtenberger, Henri. The Third Reich. Trans. Koppel S. Pinson.
    New York, 1937. Attempt to present objective interpretation of
    ideas and policies of Nazi Germany.

Meinecke, Friedrich. The German Catastrophe; Reflections and Recol-
    lections. Trans. Sidney B. Fay. Boston, 1964. Good study of back-
    ground of National Socialism and reasons for its triumph and failure.*

Mosse, George L. The Crisis of German Ideology; Intellectual Origins
    of the Third Reich. New York, 1964. Studies roots of Nazism, trac-
    ing it back to Romantic era.*

----------------, ed. Nazi Culture: Intellectual, Cultural and Social
    Life in the Third Reich. New York, 1966. Collection of materials
    to illustrate various aspects of life between 1933 and 1939.*

Namier, Sir Lewis. Diplomatic Prelude, 1938-1939 London, 1948.
    Fine analytical study of diplomacy between Munich agreement and
    outbreak of Second World War.

----------------. Europe in Decay; A Study in Disintegration, 1936-
    1940. Gloucester, Mass., 1963. Analysis of reasons for develop-
    ment of political and diplomatic affairs.

Neumann, Franz. Behemoth: The Structure and Practice of National
Socialism, 1933-1944. New York, 1963. Best general work on whole
Nazi creation.*

Rauschning, Hermann. The Revolution of Nihilism; Warning to the West.
New York, 1939. Written by former Nazi who had been forced to re-
sign from Party because opposed some of Hitler's orders. Says
Hitler's aim not peace but world domination.

Reitlinger, Gerald. The Final Solution: The Attempt to Exterminate the
Jews of Europe, 1939-1945. New York, 1953. Tries to analyze reasons and events which led to destruction of Jews.

----------------- . The S.S.: Alibi of a Nation, 1922-1945. New York.
1957. Traces S.S. from small 200 man force to one of over 500,000,
discussing major figures.

Ritter, Gerhard. The German Resistance; Carl Goerdeler's Struggle
Against Tyranny. Trans. R. T. Clark. New York, 1959. Account
of various individuals and groups who tried to resist Hitler.

Rothfels, Hans. The German Opposition to Hitler, an Appraisal. Hins-
dale, Ill., 1948. First attempt to give comprehensive analysis of
movement which ended in attempt to assassinate Hitler, July 1944.

Schoenbaum, David. Hitler's Social Revolution: Class and Status in
Nazi Germany, 1933-1939. Garden City, N. Y., 1966. Tries de-
scribe effect of Nazi Revolution on different social groups, indicating
gap between ideology and actual character.

Seydewitz, Max. Civil Life in Wartime Germany, the Story of the Home
Front. New York, 1945. Shows how Nazis worked internally.

Shirer, William L. The Rise and Fall of the Third Reich, A History of
Nazi Germany. New York, 1960. By journalist indicating most aspects of politics, diplomacy and militarism, as well as the war.*

Speer, Albert. Inside the Third Reich: Memoirs. Trans. Richard and
Clara Winston. New York, 1970. Was Hitler's architect and war
minister. Tries to emphasize his role as well as his disappoint-
ments. Much insight into Hitler's character.*

Trevor-Roper, Hugh R. The Last Days of Hitler. London, 1947. Un-
covered much first-hand material in his official study.

Vogt, Hannah. The Burden of Guilt, A Short History of Germany, 1914-1945. New York, 1964. Tries indicate to fellow countrymen what went wrong and how new society can be built on firmer foundation.*

Waite, Robert G. L. Vanguard of Nazism; the Free Corps Movement in Postwar Germany, 1918-1923. Cambridge, Mass., 1952. Important part of immediate background of National Socialism.

Wheeler-Bennett, John W. Munich, Prologue to Tragedy. New York, 1964. Access to Nuremberg documents and Czech state archives, presents study and interpretation of 5-year period prior to Munich and 5 months after.

Wiskemann, Elizabeth. The Rome-Berlin Axis; A Study of the Relations Between Hitler and Mussolini. New and revised ed. London, 1966. History of Rome-Berlin alliance from Austrian affair to war.

POSTWAR GERMANY

Abosch, Heinz. The Menace of the Miracle: Germany From Hitler to Adenauer. Trans. Douglas Garman. New York, 1963. Good general book on Postwar period.

Adenauer, Konrad. Memoirs. Trans. Beate Ruhm von Oppen. Chicago, 1966. First of three projected volumes. Gives his account of occupation and founding of Federal Republic.

Alexander, Edgar. Adenauer and the New Germany: The Chancellor of the Vanquished. Trans. Thomas E. Goldstein. New York, 1957. Explanation of the man and his role in history, showing regeneration of free Germany.

Almond, Abraham A., ed. The Struggle for Democracy in Germany. New York, 1965. 7 experts indicate background and present condition of Germany.

Bach, Julian S. America's Germany, An Account of the Occupation. New York, 1946. Correspondent for Army Talks gives detailed picture of all aspects of U.S. Zone.

Balfour, Michael L. G. West Germany. New York, 1968. Good discussion of political aspects.

Bolling, Klaus. Republic in Suspense; Politics, Parties and Personalities in Post War Germany. Trans. Jean Steinberg. New York, 1964. Account of domestic and foreign problems facing Republic.

Clay, Lucius D. _Decision in Germany_. Garden City, N. Y., 1960.
   Discussion of his work in reconstructing Germany.

Davidson, Eugene. _The Death and Life of Germany, An Account of the
   American Occupation_. New York, 1959. Chronological study of
   politics, society and economics of postwar Germany.

Dornberg, John. _The Other Germany_. Garden City, N. Y., 1968.
   Newsweek Bureau Chief for East Europe, describes various aspects
   of East Germany.

Dos Passos, John. _Tour of Duty_. Boston, 1946. Tells of his view of
   war and aftermath, December, 1944-December, 1945.

Dulles, Eleanor Lansing. _One Germany or Two; The Struggle at the
   Heart of Europe_. Stanford, Calif., 1970. Discussion of issues involved in the split and attempts to reunify Germany.

Golay, John. _The Founding of the Federal Republic of Germany_. New
   York, 1958. Best work on period since 1949. Tells of constitution-
   making and application of law.

Gottlieb, Manuel. _The German Peace Settlement and the Berlin Crisis_.
   New York, 1960. Discussion of attempts at peace and problems of
   Allied occupation of Berlin.

Grosser, Alfred. _The Colossus Again: Western Germany from Defeat
   to Rearmament_. Trans. Richard Rees. History of Western Germany, 1945-55.

----------------. _Germany in Our Time; A Political History of the
   Post War Years_. Trans. Paul Stephenson. New York, 1971. Beginning in 1945, gives account of development of Germany and its role
   in world politics.

Hanhardt, Arthur M. _The German Democratic Republic_. Baltimore,
   1968. Study of relations of German Democratic Republic with
   allies in Soviet Bloc.

Heidenheimer, Arnold J. _The Government of Germany_. New York,
   1966. Study of political development.

Jaspers, Karl. _The Future of Germany_. Trans. E. B. Ashton. Chicago, 1967. Thesis that Germany is on way to abolishing Parliamentary democracy and may be drifting toward dictatorship which
   could again threaten the peace of the world.

Landauer, Carl. Germany: Illusions and Dilemmas. New York, 1969.
Study of East and West Germany. Asks for recognition of East
Germany in return for security of West Berlin.

McClellan, Grant S. The Two Germanies. New York, 1959. Study of
development of two German states and problems involved in European politics.

Merkle, Peter H. The Origin of the West German Republic. New York,
1963. Study of political and social development of West Germany.

Mosse, William E. The European Powers and the German Question.
Attitudes of non-German great powers.

Nettl, John Peter. The Eastern Zone and Soviet Policy in Germany,
1945-50. New York, 1951. Comprehensive analysis of political,
administrative and economic developments in East German State.

Pounds, Norman J. Divided Germany and Berlin. Princeton, 1962.
Attempts to analyze major problems involved.

Richardson, James L. Germany and the Atlantic Alliance; The Inter-
action of Strategy and Politics. Cambridge, Mass., 1966. Two
themes: relationship between strategy and politics in nuclear age
and problem of tension between NATO doctrines and members' interests.

Stahl, Walter, ed. The Politics of Postwar Germany. New York, 1963.
Essays analyze success and failures of first years of West German
Republic.

Tauber, Kurt P. Beyond Eagle and Swastika; German Nationalism Since
1945. Middletown, Conn., 1967. Claims that sociopolitical conservatism still attractive to some Germans. Tries define and
analyze all aspects of this.

Thayer, Charles W. The Unquiet Germans. New York, 1957. Good
studies of leaders, especially Adenauer.

Weymar, Paul. Adenauer, His Authorized Biography. Trans. Peter de
Mendelssohn. New York, 1957. Explains regeneration of Germany
and role of Adenauer.

Willis, Frank R. The French in Germany. 1945-1949. Stanford, Calif.,
1962. Fine study of early period of French occupation.

Zink, Howard. The U.S. in Germany, 1945-1955. Princeton, 1957.
   Study of U.S. occupation policy by first Chief Historian in office of
   U.S. High Commissioner in Germany.

CULTURAL HISTORY

Anderson, Eugene N. Nationalism and the Cultural Crisis in Prussia,
   1806-1815. New York, 1966. Study of growth and influence of
   nationalism in early 19th century Germany.

Bossenbrook, William J. The German Mind. Detroit, Mich., 1961.
   Highly philosophical interpretation of German history, well-documented.

Brinton, C. Crane. Nietzsche. Cambridge, Mass., 1941. Attempts to
   place Nietzsche's work in the current opinion of the time.

Bruford, W. H. Germany in the Eighteenth Century: The Social Background of the Literary Revival. Cambridge, Eng., 1939. Study of
   various classes and conditions of living.

Epstein, Klaus. The Genesis of German Conservatism. Princeton, 1960.
   Good study of cultural and social bases of conservative thought.

Ergang, Robert R. Herder and the Foundations of German Nationalism.
   New York, 1966. Herder considered one of first of modern European writers to develop comprehensive philosophy of nationalism.

Fichte, Johann G. Addresses to the German Nation. Trans. George A.
   Kelly. New York, 1968. Important translation of work of man who
   helped to develop and influence German nationalism.

Gay, Peter. Weimar Culture: The Outsider as Insider. New York,
   1968. Analyzes cultural vitality of the German Republic.

Grunberger, Richard. The Twelve-Year Reich; A Social History of Nazi
   Germany, 1933-1945. New York, 1971. Shows how Germans lived
   and regarded selves and others from 1933-1945.

Kohn, Hans. The Mind of Germany. The Education of a Nation. New
   York, 1960. Main theme is alienation of German thought from that
   of Western Europe, beginning with wars against Napoleon.

Krieger, Leonard. The German Idea of Freedom. Boston, 1957. Freedom defined as liberalism rather than popular government.

Lewis, Beth Irwin. George Grosz: Art and Politics in the Weimar Republic. Madison, Wisc., 1971. Study of ideological motivation.

McGovern, William M. From Luther to Hitler: The History of Fascist-Nazi Political Philosophy. New York, 1941. Study of origins of two ideologies in philosophic writings from 16th century to present.

Mosse, George L. The Crisis of German Ideology; The Intellectual Origins of the Third Reich. New York, 1964. Studies roots of Nazism back to romantic era.*

Newman, Ernest. The Life of Richard Wagner. 4 vols. New York, 1933. Well-documented and factual biography.

Pundt, Alfred G. Arndt and the Nationalist Awakening in Germany. New York, 1935. Study of important figure in national development.

Snyder, Louis L. German Nationalism: The Tragedy of a People; Extremism contra Liberalism in Modern German History. Port Washington, N Y. 1969. Sees tragedy of Germany in failure of nationalism and liberalism to merge.

Thomas, Richard H. Liberalism, Nationalism, and the German Intellectuals, 1822-1847; an Analysis of the Academic and Scientific Conferences of the Period. Cambridge, Eng., 1951.

Vermeil, Edmond. Germany in the 20th Century: A Political and Cultural History of the Weimar Republic and the Third Reich. New York, 1956. Political and cultural history of the period.

Von Klemperer, Klemens. Germany's New Conservatism: Its History and Dilemma in the 20th Century. Princeton, 1957. Shows that Nazism and neo-conservatism were simultaneous movements.

MILITARY HISTORY

Addington, Larry H. The Blitzkreig Era and the German General Staff, 1865-1941. New Brunswick, N.J., 1971. Good discussion of role of General Staff in the army.

Craig, Gordon A. The Politics of the Prussian Army, 1642-1945. New York, 1956. Important study dealing with military as well as political and diplomatic issues.

Gatzke, Hans W. Stresemann and the Rearmament of Germany. Baltimore, 1954. Claims Stresemann was great statesman rather than dreamer of peace.

Gorlitz, Walter, History of the German General Staff, 1657-1945. Trans. Brian Battershaw. New York, 1953. Detailed and complete.

75757